VIII INTERNATIONAL CONGRESS OF THE INTERNATIONAL ORGANIZATION FOR MASORETIC STUDIES

Chicago 1988

THE SOCIETY OF BIBLICAL LITERATURE
MASORETIC STUDIES

Edited by
E.J. Revell

Number 6
VIII INTERNATIONAL CONGRESS
OF THE INTERNATIONAL ORGANIZATION
FOR MASORETIC STUDIES

Chicago 1988

Edited by
E.J. Revell

VIII INTERNATIONAL CONGRESS OF THE INTERNATIONAL ORGANIZATION FOR MASORETIC STUDIES

Chicago 1988

Edited by
E.J. Revell

Published by
SCHOLARS PRESS
for
The Society of Biblical Literature
and
The International Organization for Masoretic Studies

VIII INTERNATIONAL CONGRESS OF THE INTERNATIONAL ORGANIZATION FOR MASORETIC STUDIES

Chicago 1988

by
E.J. Revell

© 1990
Society of Biblical Literature

Library of Congress Cataloging in Publication Data

International Organization for Masoretic Studies. International
    Congress (8th: 1988 : Chicago, Ill.)
    VIII International Congress of the International Organization for Masoretic
    Studies : Chicago, 1988 / edited by E.J. Revell.
    p. cm. -- (Masoretic studies / The Society of Biblical
    Literature ; no. 6)
    ISBN 1-55540-387-5 (alk. paper). -- ISBN 1-55540-452-9 (pbk.)
    1. Masorah--Congresses. 2. Bible. O.T.--Manuscripts, Hebrew-
-Congresses. I. Revell, E.J. (Ernest John), 1934- . II. Title.
III. Title: 8th International Congress of the Interantional
Organization for Masoretic Studies. IV. Series: Masoretic studies :
no. 6.
BS718.I57 1988
221.4'4--dc20   90-32604
                                                                       CIP

Printed in the United States of America
on acid-free paper

TABLE OF CONTENTS

	page
Harry M. Orlinsky PREFACE	vii
Philippe Cassuto MASORETIC LISTS AND *MATRES LECTIONIS*	1
Duane L. Christensen THE MASORETIC ACCENTUAL SYSTEM AND REPEATED METRICAL REFRAINS IN NAHUM, SONG OF SONGS, AND DEUTERONOMY	31
Aron Dotan MASORETIC RUBRICS OF INDICATED ORIGIN IN CODEX LENINGRAD (B19a)	37
Ilan Eldar HEBREW READING TRADITIONS OF THE JEWISH COMMUNITIES	45
Emilia Fernández-Tejero BENEDICTI ARIAE MONTANI ... DE MAZZORETH RATIONE ATQVE VSV	65
Joseph Gutmann *MASORAH FIGURATA* IN THE *MIKDASHYAH*: The Messianic Solomonic Temple in a 14th-Century Spanish Hebrew Bible Manuscript *With six illustrations following page 77.*	71

Abraham A. Lieberman
לֹא/לוֹ: AN ANALYSIS OF A KETHIB - QERE PHENOMENON   79

Maria Teresa Ortega-Monasterio
THE LATEST SPANISH CONTRIBUTION TO MASORETIC
RESEARCH   87

E. J. Revell
CONJUNCTIVE *DAGESH*: A PRELIMINARY STUDY   95

Josep Ribera
THE BABYLONIAN MASORETIC TRADITION REFLECTED
IN THE MSS OF THE TARGUM TO THE LATTER PROPHETS   103

Milton Weinberg
A STUDY OF וַיֹּאמֶר IN THE MASORA FINALIS   111

P. C. H. Wernberg-Møller
OBSERVATIONS ON THE OLD ACCUSATIVE ENDING IN
MASORETIC HEBREW   121

PREFACE

Harry M. Orlinsky
President, IOMS

The International Organization for Masoretic Studies was founded in 1972, in conjunction with the Society for Biblical Literature (the driving force behind the First International Congress of Learned Societies in the Field of Religion). Not many of those who participated in that meeting would have believed that less than two decades later, the Organization, still in conjunction with the Society, would be publishing volume 6 in a series of Masoretic Studies. Indeed, we have done even better than this, as an additional volume has been published, outside this series. The papers read at the Fifth International Congress of the Organization (held in Salamanca in conjunction with the Eleventh Congress of the International Organization for the Study of the Old Testament) were edited by Dra. Emilia Fernández Tejero, and published as vol. 33 of *Textos y Estudios "Cardenal Cisneros"* of the Consejo Superior de Investigaciones Cientificas, Madrid, 1983, in a handsome volume entitled *ESTUDIOS MASORETICOS*. The Organization specifically, and biblical scholarship generally, are beholden to the Society for its very considerable assistance in making these publications possible.

The Eighth International Congress of the Organization took place in Chicago in November, 1988, in conjunction with the annual meeting of the Society. Fifteen papers were offered by scholars from such countries as Spain, Great Britain, Israel, France, Canada, and the United States. The range of subjects discussed embraced virtually every aspect of research in the history of the transmission of the text of the Hebrew Bible prior to the invention of printing. These papers are presented here in permanent form.

The Organization is grateful to the new editor of *Masoretic Studies*, Dr. E. J. Revell, for the responsible and effective manner in which he has brought together these papers within the confines of this volume, and to the Society for co-sponsoring the volume for publication by Scholars Press.

MASORETIC LISTS AND *MATRES LECTIONIS*

Philippe Cassuto
CATAB, Université Jean Moulin
Traduit du français par J. Mesz

This communication stems directly from the constitution of an informatic edition of the Hebraic Bible manuscripts. This edition has two essential particularities, besides its support. First of all it brings together the text of eight manuscripts and an edition of the Hebraic Bible:
- The first Isaiah scroll found at Qumran.
- The manuscript of the Prophets from the Qaraite Synagogue in Cairo.
- The so called Aleppo manuscript.
- Or. 4445 from the British Library.
- B 19a from Leningrad.
- The manuscript called Codex Reuchlinianus.
- The manuscript Paris 1-2-3 from the National Library of Paris.
- The second edition of the Biblia Rabbinica from D. Bomberg.

In this way, no one of these texts has any primacy over the others. The other characteristic is that it has integrated in the text, beside a metatext, the text's division (Parashot, middle of book, and so on ...) and the Qere, marginal notes.

While putting together this edition, one fact surprised Professor G. E. Weil and myself: the three great oriental codices, the Prophets of Cairo, Aleppo and B 19a (subsequently noted as C, A and L respectively), were absolutely identical on the level of their purely consonantal text, that is on the level of the letters other than the Matres Lectionis.

This discovery brought into question many generally accepted ideas on the transmission of the text. Outside the biblical field, one knows few examples of absolutely identical manuscripts. The idea of numerous differences between MSS of the Hebrew text of the Bible is in fact born from the great Kennicott's and De Rossi's recensions during the XVIIIth century, but our great codices go against this a priori.

This remark, which has not to be developed here, brings us to the next stage, and to recognize a certain number of differences between these codices on the level of the Matres Lectionis. After having made the most accurate inventory possible, it remained to determine if these writing differences in the Matres Lectionis were purely accidental or not. If they are not accidental, we had to determine which factors were coming into account. There is a lot at stake, one has to determine if the scribes of these manuscripts were or were not subject to errors, if yes in what measure, if not how these differences can be explained.

Part One: The data
1. The Manuscripts

Here we just take into account three manuscripts: the manuscript B 19a from the Public Library of Leningrad, the manuscript of the Prophets from Cairo, and the so called Aleppo manuscript. The manuscripts are all three linked to the name of the Ben-Asher family. This fact could have been insignificant if Maimonides had not decreed that the biblical text had to follow the reading of this family. The importance of this is proved by the fact that many practising Jews link the Aleppo manuscript directly to Maimonides, who is supposed to have used it himself. These Jews search for a prototype Ben Asher which will allow to establish this authority still more.

The manuscript of Leningrad, [L], is dated to 1009 and its discovery in the middle of the XIXth century by A. Firkowitch is directly related to Qaraism. Firkowitsch wanted so much to prove his faith in Qaraism that he even falsified some manuscripts. Thus at a distance of several centuries, one gets back to the conflict between Maimonides and the Qaraites.

As early as 1937, R. Kittel and P. Kahle used it as *the* Hebraic Bible. Although this edition was not an accurate copy of the manuscript, such was their intention. Of Leningrad two microfilms exist, one made by P. Kahle in Germany before the second world war, from which was produced the facsimile edited by Makor[1]. The other one was produced by the Leningrad Library. We have to make clear that these microfilms are unequal in quality, and it would be a good thing if a new one could be produced.

The manuscript of the Prohets from Cairo, [C], is generally dated back to 895. It is attributed directly to Moshe Ben Asher. Several microfilms of [C] exist; we have two in the CATAB, one of which was produced by P. Kahle himself. It includes the entire text of the Prophets and it appears that this volume constitutes a book by itself considering the colophon and the *masorah finalis* included in it. The Institute Arias Montano is currently working to produce a scientific edition of it and already several volumes have been published.

The so called Aleppo manuscript, the כתר ארם צובא, has suffered heavy damage during the pogrom perpetrated by the Syrians against the Jews of Aleppo in 1947. Practically the entire Pentateuch, a great deal of the Hagiographa and some folios of the Prophets are missing. It is now in Jerusalem at the Ben Zvi Institute, where it is difficult to see it.

We recall these facts, because these three manuscripts, although they really exist, are very hard to see and the researcher has to be content with reproductions that he cannot compare with the originals in case of doubt. The great researcher D. Barthélémy has thus indicated the necessity *"to raise some questions about the*

---

1. *Codex Leningrad B 19a, the earliest complete Bible manuscript*, facsimile carried out by D. S. Loewinger, Makor Press, Jerusalem, 1971.

reliability of the splendid facsimile published by the Magnes Press, the contrast achieved having required a number of interpretative interventions from the publisher".[2]

2. The collection of the data

To gather our data, we used the augmented data-base at the CATAB.[3] Indeed, instead of recording a Biblical manuscript completely, our method consists in transfering all the particulars of differences of every nature on to [L] as base text.

Thus we have checked the nearly absolute consonantal isomorphism of the four great oriental *codices*: Or.4445, [C], [A], [L]. We must however bring here a limit to the results of this work, that of human error, and it is practically certain that errors of recording slipped into our comparison.[4]

Thus we were able to make an inventory of the words whose writing differed from one manuscript to another in the *Matres Lectionis*. To classify them easily, we have distinguished between them by the only real fact which separates them: by which *Matres Lectionis* do they differ? In this way, we have the words which differ by the writing of the *waw*, of the *yod* or the *aleph*. We have found no differences in the writing of the *he*. We were basically concerned by the Prophets' text, for which we have made an inventory of 160 writing differences in the *Matres Lectionis*.

3. Minority readings, majority readings.

We have thus grouped together our data in one table arranged according to the sequential ordering of occurrence in the text of the Bible. For greater clarity, we have noted in different writing the minority reading between our three manuscripts. Majority and minority is only here a matter of a technical datum, and must not be interpreted as being more than the fact that the minority reading exists only in one manuscript, while in the two others we find the majority reading.

One does not find more than 160 divergent readings[5] in the Prophets between our three manuscripts; this number is too small to conclude on scribe errors. We would have had to have a number more in relation considering the total of possibilities of writing a word in *scriptio plena* or *defectiva*.

---

2. D. Barthélemy, *Texte, massores et fac-similé du manuscrit d'Alep*, in D. Muñoz León (éd.), *Salvación en la Palabra, ... en memoria A. Díez Macho*, Madrid, 1986, p. 62.

3. The augmented data base from the CATAB consists of seven manuscripts of the Bible: the first Isaiah scroll of Qumran (1QIsa[a]), Or. 4445, the Prophets from Cairo [C], Aleppo [A], B 19a from Leningrad [L], the Codex Reuchlinianus and manuscript Paris 1-2-3 from the National Library in Paris [P].

4. A recent comparison of the alphabetic text of the B 19a registered in the CATAB, and the one registered by the group of the professors Andersen and Forbes, revealed more than 300 differences between the two recordings.

5. This number can be compared to a number of divergences that exist between the CATAB and Andersen-Forbes.

Another observation imposes itself and will orientate our search. In these 160 divergences, 151 are bound to masoretic notes (מסורה גדולה וקטנה), either on the word in the verse itself, or in another occurrence of this same word. If we estimate that less than 5% of the words from the Hebrew Bible are object of a masoretic note, and when we see that our ratio for our divergences is 95%, we can only conclude that there is a strong connection between these notes and the writing divergences from the *Matres Lectionis*. Thus, we can already exclude the comprehension of these divergences as scribal errors.

We notice also that our 160 divergences, [L] includes 117 minority readings, [C] includes 18 and [A] includes 29. From this we can easily deduce that [C] and [A] are manuscripts very close to each other, while [L] differs more from them. We may not of course infer from this that these manuscripts belong to two different schools, and this for two essential reasons. First of all these manuscripts retain the marks of numerous emendations that we cannot date with certainty (for [L] we may not forget that it has gone through the uncareful hands of A. Firkowitsch), moreover, this small number cannot justify the existence of two schools, at the very most it indicates to us divergences in interpretation of the masoretic lists.

It is important to try to analyse the causes of these divergences, because their number will grow with time. Thus, in [P], we can count in just the Pentateuch 404 writing divergences of the *Matres Lectionis*, and near 3000 in the Prophets; this is twenty times more than the divergences between our oriental *Codices*. The same causes producing the same effects, it seems that at the time of [P] around 1286, the scribes did not understand the masoretic lists anymore, and they had to content themselves with writing them out under the form of harmonious calligraphies.

4. Data classification.

To make the analysis easier, we have classified these 160 divergences. However, these classes are artificial and have an essentially descriptive role. Thus a divergence which belongs to one class, might also be considered as belonging to another class and sometimes it is very hard to classify such divergences.

4.1. *Semantically justified divergences.*

It is a matter of an unique case where the divergence describes two manners of differentiating words which graphically look alike: the masoretes have distinguished through different methods the words ארמנות and אלמנות. We develop this case in the part reserved for analysis. It concerns only five cases.

4.2. *Divergences which put the text and the masoretic notes in contradiction*

These divergences concern a masoretic note which refutes the text, or a passage of the text that refutes a masoretic note in one or more manuscripts. This category, with 38 cases, is relatively rare. The following classes differ from this one by the fact that we cannot determine a contradiction between the literal[6] text and the masoretic

---

6. We call literal, or alphabetic, the text composed with the twenty-two letters of the Hebrew alphabet. The problem is to differentiate the vocalic literal text made up from the four *Matres Lectionis*, and the consonantal literal text made up from the other

notes. Subsequently we are in the presence of **coherent** divergences.

4.3. *Divergences due to different interpretations of the masoretic lists.*
This class is far more numerous, with 73 cases.

4.3.1. *Interpenetrations of the masoretic vocabulary.*
In 48 cases, the divergence results from an interpenetration of several masoretic lists. It happens indeed frequently that a word depends on several lists: one making a census of the *Matres Lectionis* writing, another making a census of a *Qere-Ketib* list, another making a census of a particular accentuation, etc. ...

4.3.2. *Different interpretations of the masoretic vocabulary.*
The divergence can result from the ambiguity of certain terms of the masoretic vocabulary. Thus when a word contains a *waw* and a *yod*, or two of those letters, it is difficult to know to which of them a note of the type חס or מל is related.

4.4. *Other divergences concerned with a masoretic note.*
In 29 cases of divergences, the word in question is the object of a masoretic note, but it is impossible to find the origin of the divergence, as in the previous cases.

4.5. *Unnoted divergences.*
We have also 15 cases of divergences, in which the words in question are not the object of any masoretic note. It is easy to divide this class into two: either the word in question has several written readings, or the word is an hapax and in this case it would be vain to look for an explanation.

Table 1 (summarizing section 4)

Nature of divergence		Number of cases
semanticaly justified		5
contra-textum		38
interpretation of the massoretics lists		73
list interpenetration	48	
vocabulary interpretation	25	
other divergences being object of a massoretic note		29
divergences not annotated of which 9 hapax legomena		15

---

purely consonantal letters.

Second Part: Analysis.
1. Semantically justified divergences.

It is a matter of an unique case. The words in question are: ארמנות and אלמנות, in their occurrences, in the construct state suffixed. The occurrences of אלמנות in question are shown in Table 2.

Table 2

References	L	C	A
Is 9,16	אַלְמְנֹתָיו	אַלְמְנֹתָיו	אַלְמְנֹתָיו
Jr 15,8	אַלְמְנֹתָו	אַלְמְנֹתָיו	אַלְמְנֹתָיו
		חס ק	חס ק
Ez 19,7	אַלְמְנוֹתָיו	אַלְמְנֹתָיו	אַלְמְנוֹתָיו
		ג בליש	
Ps 78,64	וְאַלְמְנֹתָיו	?	וְאַלְמְנֹתָיו
			ב חס
Jb 27,15	וְאַלְמְנֹתָיו	?	וְאַלְמְנֹתָיו
Is 13,22	בְּאַלְמְנוֹתָיו	בְּאַלְמְנוֹתָיו	בְּאַלְמְנוֹתָיו
Jr 49,11	וְאַלְמְנֹתֶיךָ	וְאַלְמְנֹתֶיךָ	וְאַלְמְנֹתֶיךָ

This table shows that, among the seven occurrences of this word, we count three divergent readings; this cannot be considered in any case as a common scribe's error, unless we consider that he had a specific psychological problem with widows.

[L] does not present any masoretic note, so the text of the manuscript is therefore coherent, except if proven the contrary. The note ב חס of [A] under Ps 78,64 suggests that the other forms bear the *scriptio plena*, it is in any case what the text of [A] indicates, in which we encounter only two forms in *scriptio defectiva* (under Ps 78,64 and Jb 27,15). The text of [C] also follows this reading.

We ask ourselves then legitimately what seems to be the reason of the divergence with [L]. It appears that the answer is given by a masoretic note from [C]:

בְּ בליש. The meaning of בליש is in general large enough, but in our particular case, the note refers to the two occurrences of אלמנות that the exegetic tradition asks us to read ארמנות (Ez 19,7 and Is 13,22). It happens that these two forms, the only ones in [L] which bear the *scriptio plena*, have the meaning of fortress, while those with the *scriptio defectiva* have the meaning of widows, cases that would be otherwise undistinguishable since they have the identical written form. Yet we have to beware of concluding that all the *scriptio plena* and *defectiva* indicate a semantic difference.

Indeed, we have just brought here the only divergence that one can understand in this manner. The other divergences have not any semantic base; in any case, we didn't make any census of them. In conclusion, we shall indicate that it would have been impossible for us to find the reason of that divergence without the masoretic note of [C].

2. Divergence bound to masoretic notes.
2.1. Contra textum.

The term itself is borrowed from the commentary on the masoretic notes written by G. E. Weil in the Biblia Hebraica Stuttgartensia. He points out that the note is in contradiction with what is actually written in the text. In any case, it applies to quantitative, not to qualitative data.

We shall present a typical example, because it involves not only marginal notes, but also notes from the Masorah Gedolah.

In Judges 7,16, [A] and [C] show the *scriptio plena* רֵיקִים, while [L] shows the *scriptio defectiva* רֵקִים. None of the three manuscripts give notes under these occurrences. We could conclude here that it is a scribal error. But one sees that this is not the case as soon as one considers the other occurrences of this word. In the following we give the table with their written form and their Masorah Qetannah:

Table 3

References	L	A	C
Ju 7,16	רֵקִים	רֵיקִים	רֵיקִים
Ju 9,4	רֵיקִיםֹ	רֵיקִיםֹ	רֵיקִיםֹ
Ju 11,3	רֵיקִים	רֵיקִים	רֵיקִים
2R 4,3	רֵקִים	רֵקִים	רֵקִים
Pr 12,11	רֵיקִים	רֵיקִים	-
Pr 28,19	רֵקִים	רֵיקִים	-
2C 13,7	רֵקִיםֹ ג חס	רֵקִיםֹ ג חס	-

On the other hand, we find in [L], under 2C 13,7 a list of Masorah Gedolah (n° 4185)[7], the text of which follows:

	רקים ג חס
2S 6,20	בהגלות נגלות
2R 4,3	כלים אל המעיטי
2C 13,7	ויקבצו עליו אנשים רקים

This last note produces thus one single list of words רקים and הרקים and indicates the defective occurrences. Indeed, the occurrence of 2S 6,20 has the definite article, while the two others do not have it.

But [L], in Judges 7,16 and in Proverbs 28,19 shows a defective form which does not appear in this list. Its text is thus contradicts the note of Masorah Qetannah ג חס that we find under 2C 13,7.

On the contrary, the text of [A] is perfectly in accordance with the notes in [L]. The confusion is certainly a matter of two interpenetrations of the masoretic lists, and not of a scribe's error.

2.2. Different interpretations of masoretic lists.

We have met two types of divergences, bound to the interpretation of masoretic notes. One is due to the fact that the note has given rise to interpenetration of two different lists related to the same word under its different forms (with or without the article, conjugated or not, in the absolute state or with a pronominal affix, etc. ...); the other is due to different interpretation of the masoretic vocabulary, depending on the manuscripts. We give now an example of each.

<u>Interpenetration of masoretic lists.</u>

Under 1S 10,5 [A] and [C] write נְבָאִים. [L] has the *scriptio plena* נְבִיאִים with the note ד׳ חס בסיפ; this contradicts the text, which has a full writing.

We could simply notice this contradiction, but it happens that the word נביא is still the object of eight divergences between our three manuscripts, which cannot be pure coincidence.

First of all, the three manuscripts have made separate lists of the occurrences of this word under its plural form preceded by the definite article for the Book of Jeremiah alone. The list of these occurrences in our three manuscripts is given in Table 4 (opposite).

First of all we have to notice that the three manuscripts repeat several times the same masoretic note: ח׳ מל בסיפ, in the Book of Jeremiah, and for this same word.

---

7. This number refers to the lists we find in the **Masorah Gedolah** published by G. E. Weil from the manuscript B 19a, in volume 1, *Les listes*, Rome, 1971.

Table 4

Références	L	A	C
Jr 5,31	הַנְּבִיאִים	הַנְּבִאִים	הַנְּבִאִים
Jr 7,25	הַנְּבִיאִים	הַנְּבִיאִים	הַנְּבִיאִים
Jr 8,1	הַנְּבִיאִים	הַנְּבִיאִים	הַנְּבִיאִים
Jr 13,13	הַנְּבִיאִים	הַנְּבִאִים	הַנְּבִיאִים
Jr 14,13	הַנְּבִאִים	הַנְּבִאִים	הַנְּבִאִים
Jr 14,14	הַנְּבִאִים֩	הַנְּבִאִים֩	הַנְּבִאִים֩
Jr 14,15	הַנְּבִאִים	הַנְּבִאִים	הַנְּבִאִים
Jr 23,15	הַנְּבִאִים	הַנְּבִאִים	הַנְּבִאִים
Jr 23,16	הַנְּבִאִים֩	הַנְּבִאִים֩	הַנְּבִאִים֩
Jr 23,21	הַנְּבִאִים	הַנְּבִאִים	הַנְּבִאִים
Jr 23,25	הַנְּבִאִים	הַנְּבִאִים	הַנְּבִאִים
Jr 23,26	הַנְּבִאִים	הַנְּבִאִים	הַנְּבִאִים
Jr 23,30	הַנְּבִאִים	הַנְּבִאִים	הַנְּבִאִים
Jr 23,31	הַנְּבִיאִם	הַנְּבִיאִם	הַנְּבִיאִם
Jr 25,4	הַנְּבִאִים	הַנְּבִאִים	הַנְּבִאִים
Jr 26,5	הַנְּבִאִים	הַנְּבִאִים	הַנְּבִאִים
Jr 26,16	הַנְּבִיאִים	הַנְּבִיאִים	הַנְּבִיאִים
Jr 27,14	הַנְּבִאִים	הַנְּבִאִים	הַנְּבִאִים
Jr 28,8	הַנְּבִיאִים	הַנְּבִיאִים	הַנְּבִיאִים
Jr 29,1	הַנְּבִיאִים֩	הַנְּבִיאִים֩	הַנְּבִיאִים֩
Jr 29,19	הַנְּבִאִים֩	הַנְּבִיאִם֩	הַנְּבִאִים֩
Jr 35,15	הַנְּבִאִים	הַנְּבִיאִם	הַנְּבִאִים
Jr 44,4	הַנְּבִיאִים	הַנְּבִיאִים	הַנְּבִיאִים

When we read the table, we count in [L] eight occurrences in *scriptio plena*, plus the occurrence הנביאם, which is the object of a specific note: ג כת כן בליש, that excludes it from this list. For the masorete of [L], the eight cases of the note apply only to the forms whose second *Yod* is written. We are thus already in the presence of two distinct lists: the list of the forms of this word in the plural preceded by the definite article in the Book of Jeremiah, and the list of plural forms of this word which second *Yod* is missing, without any distinction.

For [A], we reach the same conclusions: the occurrence in Jer 23,31 is excluded from the count and forms another separate list.

For [C], we have two solutions, either the list includes the occurrence in Jer 23,31, and we find the eight occurrences counted by this list, or else, we have to consider that the text of [C] contradicts its Masorah.

Thus we have already listed five divergences on this single word between our three manuscripts. Table 5 shows the four last ones, which concern this same word, but preceded by a conjunctive *waw*:

Table 5

Références		L	A	C
2R	23,2	וְהַכֹּהֲנִים וְהַנְּבִיאִים ג	וְהַנְּבִיאִים	וְהַכֹּהֲנִים וְהַנְּבִיאִים ל
Jr	2,8	וְהַנְּבִיאִים	וְהַנְּבִיאִים	וְהַנְּבִיאִים
Jr	4,9	וְהַנְּבִיאִים	וְהַנְּבִיאִים	וְהַנְּבִיאִים
Jr	5,13	וְהַנְּבִיאִים	וְהַנְּבִיאִים ח מל בסיפ	וְהַנְּבִיאִים
Jr	26,7	וְהַנְּבִיאִים	וְהַנְּבִיאִים	וְהַנְּבִיאִים
Jr	26,8	וְהַנְּבִיאִים ח מל בסיפ	וְהַנְּבִיאִים first written וְהַנְּבִיאִים ח מל בסיפ	וְהַנְּבִיאִים first written וְהַנְּבִיאִים erased note but still legible : ח מל בסיפ
Jr	26,11	וְהַנְּבִיאִים	וְהַנְּבִיאִים	וְהַנְּבִיאִים
Jr	27,15	וְהַנְּבִיאִים	וְהַנְּבִיאִים	וְהַנְּבִיאִים
Zk	1,5	וְהַנְּבִאִים first written וְהַנְּבִיאִים addition of the note ל חס בסיפ	lost	וְהַנְּבִיאִים

Thus we notice no less than four divergences for nine occurrences. The masoretic notes are also not very clear and the readings are uncertain.

Thus, for 2R 23,2 we find the note ג in [L] and ל in [C]. Of course this note applies to the complete expression והכהנים והנביאים. Indeed this expression appears in fact four times in the Bible, thus the texts of [L] and [C] contradict their respective notes.

The most interesting one is clearly the note ח מל בסיפ that we find in [A] and [L] and which was erased in [C], but the mark is still visible. Indeed, for [L] we count only four *plene* forms, for [A] only three (but one of the references is missing), for [C] we count also four forms, but they are not the same as for [L].

It appears evident that at the origin of this confusion is in the interpenetration of the list of occurrences from הנביאים and the list of occurrences from והנביאים. Indeed, it is the only rational way to understand the note of [L] and [A] (and the erased note of [C] which point out eight occurrences of והנביאים by assimilation with the eight occurrences of הנביאים.

This confusion derives from the growing complexity of the masoretic lists. At the beginning, the list was to be unique, but, as it was difficult to know if it concerned all the various occurrences of a particular word, two or more lists began to be used. But the heaviness of such a system quickly exerted a harmful effect, opposed to the role the masorah had fixed for itself.

<u>Divergent interpretation of the masoretic vocabulary.</u>

Another complexity, also a source of confusion, is due to the need for making clear some terms of the masoretic vocabulary. By trying to clarify them too much, the Masorah lost much of its efficiency.

We find a first example of this under Ezechiel 21,22. [L] writes וְהַנַחֹתִי without a note. Yet we have to notice that between the letters *nun* and *ḥet*, we see clearly a mark that could be read as a *yod*. [A] shows the writing וְהַנַיחֹתִי without a note, as does [C].

To have a clearer idea, here follows a table of the six occurrences of this word, with their masoretic notes in our three manuscripts.

Table 6

Références	L	A	C
Ex 33,14	וַהֲנִחֹתִי ב חס	lost	lost
2S 7,11	וַהֲנִיחֹתִי	וַהֲנִיחֹתִי	וַהֲנִיחֹתִי
Ez 5,13	וַהֲנִחוֹתִי ל כת כן	וַהֲנִחוֹתִי ל כת כן	וַהֲנִחוֹתִי ב חס
Ez 16,42	וַהֲנִחֹתִי ח	וַהֲנִחֹתִי ב חס	וַהֲנִחֹתִי ב חס
Ez 21,22	וַהֲנִחֹתִי	וַהֲנִיחֹתִי	וַהֲנִיחֹתִי
1C 22,9	וַהֲנִחוֹתִי without note	וַהֲנִיחוֹתִי ל מל	lost

When we consider this table, we see that this word admits not less than four different written forms. The note בֿ חֿס can be found in our three manuscripts, but if [L] and [A] seem to apply this note only to the written form וָהֲנֹחֹתִי, [C] applies it also to the written form וָהֲנוֹחֹתִי in Ezechiel 5,13. While [A] and [L] emphasize the unique character of this last written form.

The note of [A] under 1C 22,9 indicates that only this form is considered as absolutely *plene*. [L] here adopts another written form that, moreover, contradicts its own masoretic note from Ez 5,13.

All these divergences come from the insufficiency of the terms חס and מל, that cannot describe more than two written forms without ambiguity. In the case in which the word has a third possible written form, the masorete could note it חֿ כֿ. But in our case, the word has a fourth written form, attested in [A], thus one of the four written forms had to remain without any note. The notes in [C] show that it applies the same note to two written forms, which can lead only to the confusion that we find back in [L], with the note הֿ under Ez 16,42, that indicates thus five occurrences, when the text has really six.

Besides the divergences due to an insufficiency of the terms חס and מל the other important source of confusion is obviously the determining of the field of application of the masoretic note: does it apply to the complete biblical text, or to one of its three important parts, or to a specific book? For this reason a lot of lists were divided into smaller ones or unified in bigger ones, but as it gained in precision, the system grew heavy and became a source of confusion.

2.3. *Divergences not explained by masoretic notes.*

Certain words are the object of divergences between our three manuscripts, but they are accompanied by masoretic notes which do not contradict the text, and this forbids establishing the divergence on a logical base. Nevertheless we are beginning to see the same sources of confusion as previously.

An unusual case illustrates this confusion very well. Under Judges 18,7, [L] writes מְצָרֹים without note. [A] has the *plene* writing מְצָירֹים without note. [C] had first written מְצָרֹים and it has been corrected into מְצָירָים without note. Thus we see already all the extent of the confusion. The occurrences of this word, with their respective notes in our three manuscripts, are given in table 7 (opposite).

We count effectively in [L] no more than five defective occurrences, if we take the case of צָרְןֿ from 1R 11,33 as a specific case owing to its unusual plural ending.

We do not have the text of [A] and [C] for the occurrence of Esdras 3,7, and that keeps us from concluding definitively. The source of error comes, in my opinion, from Ju 18,7, where we have two occurrences of this word. The masorete had to ask himself if he had to count the verse and its two occurrences as one single element or as two separate elements. Indeed we find this hesitation in many masoretic notes.

Table 7

References		L	A	C
Dt	3,9	צִידֹנִים ל ראש פס	lost	lost
Ju	10,12	וְצִידוֹנִים written first וְצִידֹנִים ל מל	וְצִידוֹנִים ל מל	וְצִידוֹנִים ל מל
Ju	18,7	צִידֹנִים ה חס	צִידֹנִים ה חס	צִידֹנִים without note
Ju	18,7	מִצִּדֹנִים	מִצִּידֹנִים	מִצִּידֹנִים written first מִצִּדֹנִים
1R	5,20	כַּצִּדֹנִים ה מל	כַּצִּדֹנִים ה מל	כַּצִּדֹנִים without note
1R	11,5	צִדֹנִים ה מל	צִדֹנִים ה כת כן	צִדֹנִים ה מל
1R	11,33	צִדֹנִין ל וחס	צִדֹנִין ל	צִדֹנִין ל
Ea	3,7	לְצִדֹנִים written first לְצִידֹנִים	lost	lost

Besides this question, one other remains: from when do the successive corrections of the text of our three manuscripts date? But here, in the absence of other elements, it is for us practically impossible to give an answer. Logically one would think that the masorete himself corrected the text from his colleague the scribe of the alphabetic text, but is this really evident?

3. **Divergences that are independent from any masoretic note.**

This is the less numerous class of writing divergences from the *Matres Lectionis* between our three manuscripts. In the absence of any masoretic note, it appears difficult to understand the origin of the difference, at the very most we can sometimes conjecture certain hypotheses.

In this way, under Isaiah 17,9, [L] bears the defective writing מָעֻז without note. [A] and [C] have the *plene* writing מָעוּז without any note. We find another occurrence of this form in Ps 52,9, it has the *plene* writing in [L] and [A] without any note.

Thus we are not able to conclude anything. Only a presumption appears when we look at the occurrence of Daniel 11,10 where [L] shows מָעֻזֹּה in its text, and in the marginal note מעוז ק. But the text of [A] and [C] is missing and thus it is impossible for us to conclude.

There it was possible to us to put forward a hypothesis because of the presence of other occurrences having the same form. But this is not the case for the nine *hapax legomena* which are the object of a divergence between our three manuscripts. We give here the list of these.

Table 8

References		L	A	C
1R	6,4	אֲטֻמִים	אֲטוּמִים	אֲטוּמִים
Is	23,13	עֹרְרוּ	עוֹרְרוּ	עוֹרְרוּ
Is	29,15	יֹדְעֵנוּ	יֹדְעֵנוּ	יֹדְעֵנוּ
Is	35,7	לְמַבֻּעֵי	לְמַבּוּעֵי	לְמַבֻּעֵי
Os	7,12	אַיְסִרֵם	אַיְסִירֵם	אַיְסִירֵם
Ze	2,8	וְגִדּוּפֵי	וְגִדֻּפֵי	וְגִדּוּפֵי
Zk	5,11	מְכֻנָתָהּ	lost	מְכוּנָתָהּ
Zk	10,10	וַהֲשִׁבוֹתִים	וַהֲשִׁבוֹתִים	וַהֲשִׁבוֹתִים
Ml	1,14	וְנֹדֵר	וְנֹדֵר	וְנֹדֵר

Conclusion

We started off from a basic observation discovered during the recording of the three great oriental *codices*, called [L], [A] and [C]. These three manuscripts are almost totally isomorphic concerning their alphabetic purely consonantal text.

The problem presented was very clear. How can one explain or at least how can one understand the heteromorphy of the vocalic alphabetic text? To solve this problem we tried to classify these divergences *Matres Lectionis*, and to see which correlations we could deduce from this classification.

We have laid down as a hypothesis that the instability of this part of the text was tied up with the masoretic apparatus, and we have seen that this hypothesis was right for 95% of the registered divergences between our three manuscripts, which seems to us a satisfactory ratification of our hypothesis. As for the remaining 5%, formed exclusively by nine hapax legomena, it is highly probable that we shall be able to reduce them to the previous hypothesis.

In fact, this short study is only the reflection of the writing instability of certain letters from the Hebrew alphabet. It is true that this was the main concern of the grammarians contemporary to our manuscripts. The recognized objective of the masoretic apparatus remained unstable in the text's transmission.

The evidence of this is that practically no masoretic note concerns the writing of the consonantal alphabetic text. From this we can infer a short contribution to the history of the biblical text: at the time of our three manuscripts, the consonantal alphabetic text was perfectly steady and fixed.

Appendix

The following tables show the differences in the ues of *Matres Lectionis* between the three great oriental codices.

Références	L	C	A
Dt 30,19	הַעִידֹתִי	néant	הַעִדֹתִי

Références	L	C	A
Js 13,17	דִּיבוֹן	דִּבֹן	דִּבוֹן
Js 13,23	לְמִשְׁפְּחוֹתָם	לְמִשְׁפְּחוֹתָם	לְמִשְׁפְּחוֹתָם
Js 14,10	וּשְׁמוֹנִים	וּשְׁמוֹנִים	וּשְׁמֹנִים
Js 22,32	וַיָּשִׁבוּ	וַיָּשִׁיבוּ	וַיָּשִׁיבוּ
Js 23,7	בוֹא	בוֹא	בֹא
Js 24,3	אוֹתוֹ	אֹתוֹ	אֹתוֹ
Ju 1,3	בְּגוֹרָלִי	בְּגֹרָלִי	בְּגֹרָלִי
Ju 1,6	אוֹתוֹ	אֹתוֹ	אוֹתוֹ
Ju 1,14	לִשְׁאוֹל	לִשְׁאָל	לִשְׁאָל
Ju 1,27	יֹשֵׁב	יוֹשֵׁב	יוֹשֵׁב
Ju 7,16	רֵקִם	רֵיקִים	רֵיקִים
Ju 8,2	הֲלֹא	הֲלֹא	הֲלֹא
Ju 8,26	וְהַנְּטִפוֹת	וְהַנְּטִיפוֹת	וְהַנְּטִיפוֹת
Ju 9,6	מִלּוֹא	מִלֹּא	מִלֹּא
Ju 11,31	וְהַעֲלִיתֵהוּ	וְהַעֲלִיתִיהוּ	וְהַעֲלִיתִיהוּ
Ju 11,31	עוֹלָה	עֹלָה	עֹלָה
Ju 11,33	בּוֹאֲךָ	בּוֹאֲךָ	בֹּאֲךָ
Ju 12,11	אֵילוֹן	אֵלֹן	אֵילוֹן
Ju 12,12	אֵלוֹן	אֵלֹן	אֵילוֹן
Ju 18,7	מִצְדֹנִים	מִצִּידֹנִים	מִצִּידֹנִים
Ju 19,9	לַעֲרֹב	לַעֲרוֹב	לַעֲרוֹב

Masoretic Lists and Matres Lectionis / 17

References		L	C	A
Ju	21,12	וַיָּבִיאוּ	וַיָּבֹאוּ	וַיָּבֹאוּ
1S	1,25	וַיָּבִיאוּ	וַיָּבֵאוּ	וַיָּבֵאוּ
1S	1,28	הִשְׁאִלְתִּהוּ	הִשְׁאִלְתִּיהוּ	הִשְׁאִלְתִּיהוּ
1S	4,19	הַשְּׁמֻעָה	הַשְּׁמוּעָה	הַשְּׁמוּעָה
1S	5,2	וַיָּבִיאוּ	וַיָּבֵאוּ	וַיָּבֵאוּ
1S	10,5	נְבִיאִים	נְבִאִים	נְבִאִים
1S	17,36	הַדּוֹב	הַדֹּב	הַדֹּב
1S	17,50	וַיְמִיתֵהוּ	וַיְמִתֵהוּ	וַיְמִתֵהוּ
1S	19,9	יוֹשֵׁב	יֹשֵׁב	יֹשֵׁב
1S	20,15	תַכְרֵת	תַכְרִית	תַכְרִית
1S	31,10	וַיְשִׂמוּ	וַיָּשִׂימוּ	וַיָּשִׂימוּ
2S	10,3	חָקוֹר	חָקֹר	חָקֹר
2S	18,15	וַיְמִיתֻהוּ	וַיְמִתֻהוּ	וַיְמִתֻהוּ
2S	18,17	וַיַּשְׁלִיכוּ	וַיַּשְׁלִכוּ	וַיַּשְׁלִכוּ
2S	21,17	וַיְמִיתֻהוּ	וַיְמִתֻהוּ	וַיְמִתֻהוּ
2S	22,34	בָּמוֹתָי	בָּמֹתָי	בָּמֹתָי
2S	22,48	וּמוֹרִיד	וּמֹרִיד	וּמֹרִיד
1R	1,53	וַיּוֹרִדֻהוּ	וַיֹּרִדֻהוּ	וַיֹּרִדֻהוּ
1R	6,4	אֲטֻמִים	אֲטוּמִים	אֲטוּמִים
1R	6,29	וְתִמֹרֹת	וְתִמֹרֹת	וְתִמֹרוֹת
1R	6,32	וְתִמֹרוֹת	וְתִמֹרֹת	וְתִמֹרֹת
1R	7,30	הַכְּתֵפֹת	הַכְּתֵפֹת	הַכְּתֵפוֹת

References		L	C	A
1R	7,41	גֻלֹּת	גֻלֹּת	גֻלֹּת
1R	7,42	גֻלֹּת	גֻלֹּת	גֻלֹּת
1R	8,29	פְּתָחֹת	פְּתָחֹת	פְּתָחֹת
1R	8,52	פְּתֻחוֹת	פְּתֻחֹת	פְּתֻחֹת
1R	9,22	וְשָׁלִשָׁיו	וְשָׁלִשָׁיו	וְשָׁלִשָׁיו
1R	12,16	אֲלֵיהֶם	אֲלֵהֶם	אֲלֵהֶם
1R	14,7	הֲרִימֹתִיךָ	הֲרִמֹתִיךָ	הֲרִמֹתִיךָ
1R	20,34	וְחוּצוֹת	וְחוּצוֹת	וְחֻצוֹת
1R	21,9	וְהוֹשִׁיבוּ	וְהֹשִׁיבוּ	וְהֹשִׁיבוּ
1R	22,16	מַשְׁבִּעֶךָ	מַשְׁבִּיעֶךָ	מַשְׁבִּיעֶךָ
1R	22,26	וַהֲשִׁיבֵהוּ	וַהֲשִׁבֵהוּ	וַהֲשִׁיבֵהוּ
1R	22,27	וְהַאֲכִילֻהוּ	וְהַאֲכִלֻהוּ	וְהַאֲכִלֻהוּ
1R	22,49	אוֹפִירָה	אֹפִירָה	אֹפִירָה
2R	2,18	הֲלוֹא	הֲלֹא	הֲלֹא
2R	7,5	וַיָּקוּמוּ	וַיָּקֻמוּ	וַיָּקֻמוּ
2R	8,23	הֲלוֹא	הֲלֹא	הֲלֹא
2R	10,17	הִשְׁמִידוֹ	הִשְׁמְדוֹ	הִשְׁמְדוֹ
2R	12,21	הַיּוֹרֵד	הַיֹּרֵד	הַיֹּרֵד
2R	13,6	מֵחַטֹּאות	מֵחַטֹּאת	מֵחַטֹּאת
2R	15,25	וַיְמִיתֵהוּ	וַיְמִתֵהוּ	disparu
2R	18,17	כּוֹבֵס	כּוֹבֵס	כֹּבֵס
2R	18,29	יַשִּׁיא	יַשִּׁא	יַשִּׁא
2R	18,31	בּוֹרוֹ	בֹּרוֹ	בֹּרוֹ

References		L	C	A
2R	24,11	נְבוּכַדְנָאצַּר	נְבֻכַדְנָאצַר	נְבֻכַדְנֶאצַּר
Is	3,19	הַנְּטִיפוֹת	הַנְּטִפוֹת	הַנְּטִפוֹת
Is	5,22	גִּבּוֹרִים	גִּבֹּרִים	גִּבּוֹרִים
Is	9,16	אַלְמְנֹתָיו	אַלְמְנוֹתָיו	אַלְמְנוֹתָיו
Is	17,9	מָעוּזּוֹ	מָעוּזּוֹ	מָעוּזּוֹ
Is	17,14	לְבֹזְזֵינוּ	לְבֹזְזֵנוּ	לְבֹזְזֵנוּ
Is	23,13	עֹרְרוּ	עוֹרְרוּ	עוֹרְרוּ
Is	24,3	תִּבּוֹז	תִּבֹּז	תִּבֹּז
Is	25,1	מֵרָחוֹק	מֵרָחֹק	מֵרָחֹק
Is	26,9	אֲנִיתִיךָ	אִוִּיתִיךָ	אִוִּיתִיךָ
Is	29,15	יוֹדְעֵנוּ	יֹדְעֵנוּ	יֹדְעֵנוּ
Is	29,16	לְיוֹצְרוֹ	לְיֹצְרוֹ	לְיֹצְרוֹ
Is	33,4	שׁוֹקֵק	שֹׁקֵק	שֹׁקֵק
Is	35,7	לְמַבּוּעֵי	לְמַבָּעֵי	לְמַבּוּעֵי
Is	36,22	הַסּוֹפֵר	הַסֹּפֵר	הַסֹּפֵר
Is	41,5	וְיִירָאוּ	וְיִירָאוּ	וְיִירָאוּ
Is	42,4	יְיַחֵילוּ	יְיַחֵלוּ	יְיַחֵלוּ
Is	48,15	הֲבִיאֹתָיו	הֲבִאֹתָיו	הֲבִאֹתָיו
Is	49,5	יֹצְרִי	יוֹצְרִי	יוֹצְרִי
Is	49,13	וַעֲנִיָּו	וַעֲנִיָּו	וַעֲנִיָּו
Is	49,17	וּמַחֲרְבַיִךְ	וּמַחֲרִיבַיִךְ	וּמַחֲרִיבַיִךְ
Is	49,19	הֲרִסֹתַיִךְ	הֲרִסֻתֵךְ	הֲרִסֻתֵךְ
Is	57,2	מִשְׁכְּבוֹתָם	מִשְׁכְּבֹתָם	מִשְׁכְּבוֹתָם

References	L	C	A
Is 58,13	חֲפָצֶיךָ	חֶפְצְךָ	חֶפְצֶךָ
Is 59,7	מַחְשְׁבוֹתֵיהֶם	מַחְשְׁבֹתֵיהֶם	מַחְשְׁבֹתֵיהֶם
Is 59,19	וְיִירְאוּ	וְיִרְאוּ	וְיִרְאוּ
Is 65,3	אוֹתִי	אֹתִי	אֹתִי
Jr 2,8	וְהַנְּבִיאִים	וְהַנְּבִיאִים	וְהַנְּבִיאִים
Jr 2,11	הַהֵימִיר	הַהֵמִיר	הַהֵימִיר
Jr 2,21	שֹׂרֵק	שׂוֹרֵק	שֹׂרֵק
Jr 2,36	תֵּבוֹשִׁי	תֵּבֹשִׁי	תֵּבֹשִׁי
Jr 4,3	קוֹצִים	קֹצִים	קֹצִים
Jr 4,9	וְהַנְּבִיאִים	וְהַנְּבִאִים	וְהַנְּבִאִים
Jr 4,19	אֹחֲרִישׁ	אַחֲרִשׁ	אַחֲרִשׁ
Jr 5,12	לֹא־הוּא	לוֹא־הוּא	לוֹא־הוּא
Jr 5,17	בּוֹטֵחַ	בּוֹטֵחַ	בֹּטֵחַ
Jr 5,24	וְלֹא	וְלוֹא	וְלוֹא
Jr 5,31	הַנְּבִיאִים	הַנְּבִאִים	הַנְּבִאִים
Jr 8,5	בַּתַּרְמִית	בַּתַּרְמִת	בַּתַּרְמִת
Jr 8,9	הֹבִישׁוּ	הֹבִשׁוּ	הֹבִשׁוּ
Jr 10,18	וַהֲצֵרוֹתִי	וַהֲצֵרוֹתִי	וַהֲצֵרֹתִי
Jr 12,1	אוֹתָךְ	אֹתָךְ	אֹתָךְ
Jr 13,13	הַנְּבִיאִים	הַנְּבִאִים	הַנְּבִאִים
Jr 15,8	אַלְמְנֹתָו	אַלְמְנוֹתָו	אַלְמְנוֹתָו
Jr 20,10	שְׁלוֹמִי	שְׁלֹמִי	שְׁלֹמִי

References	L	C	A
Jr 26,6	גּוֹיֵי	גּוֹיֵ	גּוֹיֵ
Jr 26,8	וְהַנְּבִאִים	וְהַנְּבִיאִים	וְהַנְּבִיאִים
Jr 29,19	הַנְּבִאִים	הַנְּבִאִים	הַנְּבִיאִים
Jr 35,15	הַנְּבִאִים	הַנְּבִאִים	הַנְּבִיאִים
Jr 38,22	אֹמְרוֹת	אֹמְרֹת	אֹמְרֹת
Jr 49,11	וְאַלְמְנֹתֶיךָ	וְאַלְמְנֹתֶיךָ	וְאַלְמְנוֹתֶיךָ
Jr 49,20	אִם־לֹא[1]	אִם־לוֹא	אִם־לוֹא
Jr 50,39	דּוֹר וָדוֹר	דּוֹר וָדֹר	דּוֹר וָדֹר
Jr 51,16	וַיֹּצֵא	וַיֹּצֵא	וַיֹּצֵא
Jr 52,2	יְהוֹיָקִים	יְהוֹיָקִם	יְהוֹיָקִם
Ez 3,2	וַיַּאֲכִלֵנִי	וַיַּאֲכִלֵנִי	וַיַּאֲכִלֵנִי
Ez 7,12	וְהַמּוֹכֵר	וְהַמֹּכֵר	וְהַמֹּכֵר
Ez 7,13	הַמּוֹכֵר	הַמֹּכֵר	הַמֹּכֵר
Ez 7,27	אוֹתָם	אֹתָם	אֹתָם
Ez 11,24	וַתְּבִיאֵנִי	וַתְּבִיאֵנִי	וַתְּבִיאֵנִי
Ez 16,4	אֹתָךְ	אוֹתָךְ	אוֹתָךְ
Ez 16,22	עֵרֹם	עֵירֹם	עֵירֹם
Ez 16,39	אוֹתָךְ	אֹתָךְ	אֹתָךְ
Ez 21,22	וַהֲנִחֹתִי	וַהֲנִיחֹתִי	וַהֲנִיחֹתִי
Ez 21,35	מְכֻרוֹתַיִךְ	מְכֻרֹתַיִךְ	מְכוּרֹתַיִךְ
Ez 24,24	כְּבֹאָהּ	בְּבוֹאָהּ	בְּבוֹאָהּ

---

[1] אִם־לֹא יִסְחָבוּם

References		L	C	A
Ez	29,1	הָעֲשִׂירִית	הָעֲשִׂירִית	הָעֲשִׂרִית
Ez	30,4	יְסוֹדֹתֶיהָ	יְסֹדוֹתֶיהָ	יְסֹדוֹתֶיהָ
Ez	37,6	גִּדִים	גִּידִים	גִּידִים
Ez	38,13	כְּפִרֶיהָ	כְּפִירֶיהָ	כְּפִירֶיהָ
Ez	40,7	אוּלָם	אוּלָם	אֵלָם
Ez	40,16	וְחַלֹנוֹת [1]	חַלוֹנוֹת	חַלוֹנוֹת
Ez	42,5	וּמֵהַתִּכֹנוֹת	וּמֵהַתִּכוֹנוֹת	וּמֵהַתִּכוֹנוֹת
Ez	43,5	וַתְּבִאֵנִי	וַתְּבִאֵנִי	וַתְּבִאֵנִי
Ez	44,3	אֵלָם	אֵלָם	אוּלָם
Ez	44,11	הָעֹלָה	הָעוֹלָה	הָעוֹלָה
Ez	46,21	וַיַּעֲבִירֵנִי	וַיַּעֲבְרֵנִי	וַיַּעֲבְרֵנִי
Os	2,17	עֲלוֹתָהּ	עֲלוֹתָהּ	עֲלוֹתָהּ
Os	3,5	דָּוִד	דָּוִיד	דָּוִיד
Os	6,3	מוֹצָאוֹ	מֹצָאוֹ	מֹצָאוֹ
Os	7,12	אִסְּרֵם	אִיסִרֵם	אִיסִרֵם
Am	1,10	אַרְמְנוֹתֶיהָ	אַרְמְנוֹתֶיהָ	אַרְמְנוֹתֶיהָ
Am	5,27	וְהִגְלֵיתִי	וְהִגְלֵיתִי	וְהִגְלֵיתִי
Mi	5,4	בְּאַרְמְנוֹתֵינוּ	בְּאַרְמְנוֹתֵינוּ	בְּאַרְמְנוֹתֵינוּ
Mi	6,2	מֹסְדֵי	מֹסְדֵי	מֹסְדֵי
Nh	2,4	פְּלָדוֹת	פְּלָדוֹת	פְּלָדֹת
Hb	2,2	כָּתוֹב	כְּתֹב	כְּתֹב

---

[1] וְחַלֹנוֹת אֲטֻמוֹת

Masoretic Lists and Matres Lectionis / 23

Références		L	C	A
Hb	2,5	בּוֹגֵד	בֹּגֵד	בֹּגֵד
Ze	2,8	וְגִדּוּפֵי	וְגִדּוּפֵי	וְגִדֻּפֵי
Zk	1,5	וְהַנְּבִיאִים	וְהַנְּבִאִים	disparu
Zk	1,17	תְּפוּצֶינָה	תְּפוּצֶנָה	disparu
Zk	5,11	מְכוּנָתָהּ	מְכֻנָתָהּ	disparu
Zk	8,19	טוֹבִים	טֹבִים	טֹבִים
Zk	10,10	וַהֲשִׁיבוֹתִים׳	וַהֲשִׁבוֹתִים׳	וַהֲשִׁבוֹתִים׳
Ml	1,8	תַּגִּשׁוּן	תַגִּשׁוּן	תַגִּשׁוּן
Ml	1,14	וְנוֹדֵר	וְנֹדֵר	וְנֹדֵר
Ml	3,4	קַדְמֹנִיּוֹת	קַדְמֹנִיֹּת	קַדְמֹנִיֹּת

References		L	A	C
1C	2,13	הַשְּׁלִשִׁי	הַשְּׁלִישִׁי	néant
1C	2,38	הֹלִיד	הֹלִיד	néant
1C	4,2	הוֹלִיד	הֹלִיד	néant
1C	4,8	וּמִשְׁפָּחוֹת	וּמִשְׁפַּחַת	néant
1C	5,25	אֲבוֹתֵיהֶם	אֲבֹתֵיהֶם	néant
1C	6,4	לַאֲבוֹתֵיהֶם	לַאֲבֹתֵיהֶם	néant
1C	6,48	זְבוּלֻן	זְבֻלוּן	néant
1C	6,62	זְבֻלֻן	זְבֻלוּן	néant
1C	9,41	פִּיתוֹן	פִּיתֹן	néant
1C	11,10	הַגִּבּוֹרִים	הַגִּבֹּרִים	néant
1C	11,42	שְׁלוֹשִׁים	שְׁלֹשִׁים	néant
1C	20,4	מִילְדֵי	מִילִדֵי	néant
1C	23,15	גֵּרְשֹׁם	גֵּרְשׁוֹם	néant
1C	23,23	שְׁלֹשָׁה	שְׁלוֹשָׁה	néant
1C	23,24	אֲבֹתֵיהֶם	אֲבוֹתֵיהֶם	néant
1C	23,27	הָאַחֲרֹנִים	הָאַחֲרוֹנִים	néant
1C	25,4	מַחֲזִיאוֹת	מַחֲזִיאֹת	néant
1C	29,21	אֵילִים	אֵלִים	néant
2C	6,28	אוֹיְבָיו	אֹיְבָיו	néant
2C	6,42	מְשִׁיחֶיךָ	מְשִׁיחֶךָ	néant
2C	7,3	וְהוֹדוֹת	וְהֹדוֹת	néant
2C	8,14	וְהַשּׁוֹעֲרִים	וְהַשֹּׁעֲרִים	néant

References		L	A	C
2C	10,4	מֵעֲבֹדַת	מֵעֲבוֹדַת	néant
2C	11,11	הַמְצֵרוֹת	הַמְצוּרוֹת	néant
2C	14,10	לַעְזוֹר	לַעְזוֹר	néant
2C	15,5	יוֹשְׁבֵי	יֹשְׁבֵי	néant
2C	15,10	הַשְּׁלִשִׁי	הַשְּׁלִשִׁי	néant
2C	22,9	וַיְמִתָהוּ	וַיְמִיתָהוּ	néant
2C	23,18	פְּקֻדֹּת	פְּקֻדּוֹת	néant
2C	25,24	אֹצְרוֹת	אוֹצְרוֹת	néant
2C	28,13	חַטֹּאתֵינוּ	חַטֹּאתֵנוּ	néant
2C	28,23	אוֹתָם	אֹתָם	néant
2C	31,1	הַמִּזְבְּחֹת	הַמִּזְבְּחוֹת	néant
2C	32,26	וְיֹשְׁבֵי	וְיוֹשְׁבֵי	néant
2C	32,28	לָאֱרוֹת	לָאֱרֹת	néant
2C	34,28	קִבְרֹתֶיךָ	קִבְרוֹתֶיךָ	néant
2C	34,33	הַתּוֹעֵבוֹת	הַתֹּעֵבוֹת	néant
2C	35,5	לְפִלַגּוֹת	לְפִלְגוֹת	néant
Ps	5,10	גְּרוֹנָם	גְּרֹנָם	néant
Ps	33,7	בְּאוֹצָרוֹת	בְּאֹצָרוֹת	néant
Ps	35,6	חֲלַקְלַקּוֹת	חֲלַקְלַקֹּת	néant
Ps	35,21	עֵינֵינוּ	עֵינֵנוּ	néant
Ps	42,6	הוֹחִילִי	הוֹחִלִי	néant
Ps	45,18	יְהוֹדֻךָ	יְהוֹדוּךָ	néant

References	L	A	C
Ps 54,2	בְּבֹוא	בְּבֹא	néant
Ps 59,15	וְיָשׁוּבוּ	וְיָשֻׁבוּ	néant
Ps 63,3	חֲזִיתִיךָ	חֲזִיתִךָ	néant
Ps 64,5	לִירוֹת	לִירֹת	néant
Ps 65,11	גְּדוּדֶיהָ	גְּדוּדֶהָ	néant
Ps 66,15	מֵחִים	מֵיחִים	néant
Ps 67,5	מִישׁוֹר	מִישֹׁר	néant
Ps 67,8	אֹתוֹ	אוֹתוֹ	néant
Ps 68,21	תּוֹצָאוֹת	תֹּצָאוֹת	néant
Ps 76,3	סֻכּוֹ	סוּכּוֹ	néant
Ps 76,12	יוֹבִילוּ	יֹבִילוּ	néant
Ps 78,4	וְנִפְלְאוֹתָיו	וְנִפְלְאֹתָיו	néant
Ps 83,12	נְדִיבֵמוֹ	נְדִיבֵימוֹ	néant
Ps 83,12	נְסִיכֵמוֹ	נְסִיכֵימוֹ	néant
Ps 87,4	וְצוֹר	וְצֹר	néant
Ps 89,16	יוֹדְעֵי	יֹדְעֵי	néant
Ps 89,18	וּבִרְצֹנְךָ	וּבִרְצוֹנְךָ	néant
Ps 89,18	קַרְנֵנוּ	קַרְנֵינוּ	néant
Ps 89,23	יַשִּׁא	יַשִּׁיא	néant
Ps 104,9	יְשׁוּבוּן	יְשֻׁבוּן	néant
Ps 116,6	דַּלּוֹתִי	דַּלֹּתִי	néant
Ps 135,6	תְּהוֹמוֹת	תְּהֹמוֹת	néant
Ps 135,9	אֹתוֹת	אוֹתֹת	néant

References	L	A	C
Ps 139,20	נָשֻׂא	נָשׂוּא	néant
Ps 143,3	הוֹשִׁיבַנִי	הוֹשְׁבַנִי	néant
Ps 150,4	וְעוּגָב	וְעֻגָב	néant
Jb 3,7	תָּבֹא	תָּבוֹא	néant
Jb 5,12	תַּעֲשֶׂינָה	תַּעֲשֶׂנָה	néant
Jb 5,12	תּוּשִׁיָּה	תֻּשִׁיָּה	néant
Jb 10,22	עֵיפָתָה	עֵפָתָה	néant
Jb 14,5	יַעֲבוֹר	יַעֲבֹר	néant
Jb 15,11	תַּנְחֻמוֹת	תַּנְחֻמֹות	néant
Jb 16,19	בַּמְּרוֹמִים	בַּמְּרֹמִים	néant
Jb 20,12	לְשׁוֹנוֹ	לְשֹׁנוֹ	néant
Jb 20,15	יוֹרִשֶׁנּוּ	יֹרִשֶׁנּוּ	néant
Jb 20,22	תְּבוֹאֶנּוּ	תְּבֹאֶנּוּ	néant
Jb 22,15	תִּשְׁמוֹר	תִּשְׁמֹר	néant
Jb 22,28	אוֹמֶר	אֹמֶר	néant
Jb 24,4	אֶבְיוֹנִים	אֶבְיֹנִים	néant
Jb 26,13	בָּרִיחַ	בָּרִחַ	néant
Jb 36,10	יָשֻׁבוּן	יְשׁוּבוּן	néant
Jb 37,8	וַתָּבֹא	וַתָּבוֹא	néant
Jb 37,15	וְהוֹפִיעַ	וְהֹפִיעַ	néant
Jb 38,22	וְאֹצְרוֹת	וְאוֹצְרֹות	néant
Jb 39,7	נֹגֵשׂ	נֹגֵשׂ	néant

References		L	A	C
Jb	40,16	וְאֹנוֹ	וְאוֹנוֹ	néant
Jb	40,18	נְחוּשָׁה	נְחֻשָׁה	néant
Jb	40,26	אַגְמוֹן	אַגְמֹן	néant
Jb	40,26	תְּקוֹב	תִּקֹּב	néant
Jb	41,8	יָבוֹא	יָבֹא	néant
Pr	1,3	וּמֵישָׁרִים	וּמֵשָׁרִים	néant
Pr	1,9	לְגַרְגְּרֹתֶיךָ	לְגַרְגְּרֹתֶךָ	néant
Pr	4,15	וַעֲבוֹר	וַעֲבֹר	néant
Pr	5,22	עֲווֹנֹתָיו	עֲוֹנֹתָיו	néant
Pr	7,22	יָבוֹא	יָבֹא	néant
Pr	8,2	מְרוֹמִים	מְרֹמִים	néant
Pr	8,15	וְרוֹזְנִים	וְרֹזְנִים	néant
Pr	8,27	בְּחוּקוֹ	בְּחֻקוֹ	néant
Pr	10,12	תְּעוֹרֵר	תְּעֹרֵר	néant
Pr	11,3	בּוֹגְדִים	בֹּגְדִים	néant
Pr	11,24	וְחוֹשֵׂךְ	וְחֹשֵׂךְ	néant
Pr	11,29	עוֹכֵר	עֹכֵר	néant
Pr	12,1	וְשֹׂנֵא	וְשׂוֹנֵא	néant
Pr	13,18	וְשׁוֹמֵר	וְשֹׁמֵר	néant
Pr	17,23	מֵחֵיק	מֵחֵק	néant
Pr	18,11	בְּמַשְׂכִּיתוֹ	בְּמַשְׂכֻּתוֹ	néant
Pr	21,6	אוֹצָרוֹת	אֹצָרוֹת	néant

References	L	A	C
Pr 22,20	בְּמוֹעֵצֹת	בְּמֹעֵצֹת	néant
Pr 23,7	אֱכָל	אֱכוֹל	néant
Pr 26,27	יִפֵּל	יִפּוֹל	néant
Pr 26,27	וְגֵלֵל	וְגֹלֵל	néant
Pr 28,15	מֹשֵׁל	מוֹשֵׁל	néant
Pr 28,19	רֵקִים	רֵיקִים	néant
Pr 30,17	וְתָבֻז	וְתָבֻז	néant
Rt 1,5	וַיָּמוּתוּ	וַיָּמֻתוּ	néant
Rt 1,17	יֹסִיף	יוֹסִיף	néant
Rt 1,19	בֹּאֲנָה	בוֹאֲנָה	néant
Rt 1,19	כְּבֹאֲנָה	כְּבוֹאֲנָה	néant
Rt 2,14	הַקּוֹצְרִים	הַקֹּצְרִים	néant
Ct 2,14	הַשְׁמִיעִינִי	הַשְׁמִיעִנִי	néant
Ct 2,15	שׁוּעָלִים	שֻׁעָלִים	néant
Ct 2,15	שׁוּעָלִים	שֻׁעָלִים	néant
Ct 3,6	מוֹר	מֹר	néant

Divergences concernant la matres lectionis Aleph.

References		L	A	C
Js	17,15	וּבֵרֵאתָ֫	וּבֵרֵאתָ֫	וּבֵאֵרְתָ֫
Js	21,10	רִיאשֹׁנָה	רִיאשֹׁנָה	רִאשֹׁנָה
		ל חס כן	ל חס י	ל מל
Ez	17,6	פֹּארֹות	פֹּראֹות	פֹּארֹות
Ez	31,8	כְּפֹארֹתָיו	כְּפֹּראֹתָיו	כְּפֹּראֹתָיו
		ל	ל	ל
Ez	31,12	פֹּארֹתָיו	פֹּראֹתָיו	פֹּראֹתָיו
Ez	31,13	וְאֶל פֹּארֹות	וְאֶל פֹּראֹתָיו	וְאֶל פֹּראֹתָיו
		ל	ל	ל

THE MASORETIC ACCENTUAL SYSTEM AND REPEATED METRICAL REFRAINS IN NAHUM, SONG OF SONGS, AND DEUTERONOMY

Duane L. Christensen
American Baptist Seminary of the West
and Graduate Theological Union

In a paper presented at the Ninth World Congress of Jewish Studies in 1985,[1] I noted the appearance of what I called a repeated "metrical refrain" in Deuteronomy 12. Using a method of prosodic analysis which combines the counting of morae with a study of the distribution of disjunctive accents, as indicated in the Masoretic accentual system, I noted an interesting pattern in regards the metrical configuration /4:6:6:4/ or /6:4:4:6/ of accentual stress units in Deut. 12:2-3, 6-7 and 25-27. The /6:4:4:6/ structure in 12:2-3 functions as a sort of opening "refrain", which is repeated twice at the center of similar concentric metrical entities in 12:4-9 and 12:23-28 as follows:[2]

Deut. 12:2-3   /6:4:4:6/

Deut. 12:4-9   /7:5/4:6:6:4/5:7/

Deut. 12:23-28   /5:7/4:6:6:4/7:5/

At the time I was aware of a similar phenomenon in Deut. 13-14, where the opening /4:8:8:4/ metrical unit (13:2-4) be-comes a "refrain" which is repeated three more times in 13:7-8, 13:17b-19; and 14:24b-26. Though the positioning of this "refrain" at

---

1. D. L. Christensen, "The *Numeruswechsel* in Deuteronomy 12," *Proceedings of the Ninth World Congress of Jewish Studies*, Division A: The Period of the Bible (Jerusalem: World Union of Jewish Studies, 1986): 61-68.

2. Ibid., p. 67.

the center of concentric metrical configurations is not as clearly evident as its counterpart in Deut. 12, the situation was close enough to merit further investigation.

For a "Symposium on the Song of Songs" at the Society of Biblical Liberature in 1985,[3] I prepared a detailed prosodic study, which revealed an interesting repetition of these same two "metrical refrains". The opening metrical unit in Song of Songs 1:2-4 scans /4:6:6:4/ in accentual stress units, which is repeated twice in the following section in carefully balanced positions within 1:7-2:4 as follows:

$$/\underline{6{:}4{:}4{:}6}/8{:}4/6{:}6/4{:}8/\underline{4{:}6{:}6{:}4}/$$

The center of this metrical configuration (1:12-24), which may be scanned either /6:6/ or /4:4:4/, is framed by an /8:4//4:8/ structure, which is in turn repeated three times in 4:3-6:5, where it appears first as the center of a metrical configuration in 4:1-5:1a as follows:

$$/9{:}4{:}4{:}9/7/\underline{8{:}4{:}4{:}8}/7/9{:}4{:}4{:}9/$$

This "metrical refrain" in turn is used as a frame around the center of another configuration in 5:13-6:5 as follows:

$$/\underline{8{:}4{:}4{:}8}/4{:}4{:}4{:}4/\underline{8{:}4{:}4{:}8}/$$

A subsequent study of the so-called "Acrostic of Nahum", which was published in 1987,[4] revealed a similar structure for Nahum 1:1-10 as follows:

$$/8{:}4/5{:}5/\underline{8{:}4{:}4{:}8}/5{:}5/4{:}8/$$

---

3. The paper, "The Prosodic Structure of the Song of Songs", was presented November 25, 1985, in Anaheim, California, as part of a Symposium on the Song of Songs in the Biblical Hebrew Poetry Section of the Society of Biblical Literature. Other participants included Robert Alter, Michael V. Fox, David Noel Freedman, Roland E. Murphy, Marvin H. Pope, and Jack Sasson.

4. D. L. Christensen, The Acrostic of Nahum Once Again: A Prosodic Analysis of Nahum 1,1-10," *ZAW* 99 (1987): 409-15.

This /8:4:4:8/ unit at the center of the opening metrical structure in 1:1-10 is found again at the center of another configuration in 2:1-10, which scans as follows:

/5:4/7:8/8:4:4:8/8:7/4:5/

Its variant form /4:8:8:4/ appears again in 2:12-14a as the opening section of the second half of the book of Nahum

Further observations of note are in order about these repeated "metrical refrains" in Nahum. In terms of total mora-count the three occurrences of /8:4:4:8/ are 155, 151, and 157 morae respectively. The total mora-count for the three occurrences of a third "metrical refrain" which scanned /4:9:9:4/ or /9:4:4:9/ units are 162, 169, 167 morae respectively:

Nahum 1:11-14   /4:9:9:4/

Nahum 2:14b-3:5   /8:5/9:4:4:9/5:8/

Nahum 3:14-19   /4:9/6:4:4:6/9:4/

In short, these two "metrical refrains" appear at least three times each in Nahum and are remarkably consistent in both length and rhythmic structure, suggesting the possibility of repeated musical elements in the original performance of the text in ancient Israel.

Prosodic analysis of Deuteronomy, Song of Songs, and Nahum suggests that the Masoretic tradition is remarkably well preserved in these particular books. The reason for the absence of any serious textual corruptions here is probably the simple fact that we are dealing in each case with a rhythmic, musical composition. It was the memory of the musical rhythm to which the text was sung (or chanted) that served to preserve the text itself in its original form.

As Thrasybulos Georgiades has shown for classical Greek, music and language are not separate categories in the study of ancient texts.[5]

For the ancient Greeks, music existed primarily as verse. The Greek verse line was a linguistic and simultaneously a musical reality. The connecting element, common to both language and music, was rhythm. A verse line in a modern

---

5. T. Georgiades, *Music and Language: The Rise of Western Music as Exemplified in Settings of the Mass*, trans. by M. L. Göllner (Cambridge: Cambridge University Press, 1982): 4.

Western language -- German, for example -- can, to be sure, establish an order in the succession of accents which, proceeding from language, is also binding for the music . . . It cannot, however, by itself determine all aspects of the musical rhythm. For this Western verse line is not a musical but rather a linguistic form. For that reason it can be set to music in various ways . . . The ancient Greek verse line behaved differently. Here the musical rhythm was contained within the language itself.

A somewhat analogous situation apparently existed for ancient Hebrew. The rhythmic structure of the biblical text is reflected in the Masoretic accentual system, which incidentally is still used to present that text in musical form within the several canting traditions of Judaism. A careful examination of this rhythmic structure has much to contribute in terms of understanding the meaning of the text as well.

The rather elegant metrical structure of the book of Nahum, in particular, argues strongly for the musical performance of this text within the cultic life of ancient Israel, much like the Song of Songs, as I have argued elsewhere.[6] In short, the book of Nahum is a liturgical composition. It is the Day of Yahweh, as both F. C. Fensham and Kevin Cathcart have noted,[7] that provides the original setting for the book. The Holy War in ancient Israel, particularly in the premonarchic period, was a celebrated event, which F. M. Cross has described as the "Ritual conquest".[8] The Exodus-Conquest of the past was projected into the present and the future in cultic celebration, within the festal life of ancient Israel. The book of Nahum, like most of the oracles against foreign nations in the prophetic literature of the Hebrew Bible,[9] is to be understood within this Holy War tradition. As Kevin Cathcart put it,[10]

---

6. D. L. Christensen, "The Book of Nahum as a Liturgical Composition: A Prosodic Analysis," *JETS* (forthcoming).

7. F. C. Fensham, "Legal Activities of the Lord According to Nahum, "*Biblical Essays 1969: OTWSA* 12 (1969):13-20; and K. J. Cathcart, "The Divine Warrior and the War of Yahweh in Nahum," in *Biblical Studies in Contemporary Thought*, ed. Miriam Ward (Trinity College Biblical Institute; Greeno, Haddon & Co., Ltd., 1978):68-76.

8. F. M. Cross, *Canaanite Myth and Hebrew Epic* (Cambridge, MA: Harvard University Press, 1973): 99-111.

9. See D. L. Christensen, *Transformations of the War Oracle in Old Testament Prophecy: Studies in the Oracles Against the Nations* (Harvard Dissertations in Religion 3; Missoula: Scholars Press, 1975).

10. K. J. Cathcart, "The Divine Warrior," p. 76; who is quoting P. D. Miller, *The Divine Warrior in Early Israel* (Harvard Semitic Monographs 5; Cambridge: Harvard University Press, 1965): 174.

In Nahum, *'l nqm*, "the avenging God", is the one who carries out the curses as punishment of the Assyrians, to save Israel. As the Divine Warrior he wages a war against these Assyrians; as king he topples the king of Nineveh from his throne and asserts his kingship, for "it is the establishment of Yahweh's eternal rule and sovereignty that is the ultimate goal of Yahweh's wars".

We may now be in a position to recover, at least in part, some of the details of the ancient cultic experiences in which the Holy War traditions were transmitted, through careful study of the Masoretic accentual system. As Suzanne Haïk-Vantoura has noted, the Masoretes did not invent the musical tradition reflected in their sophisticated system of notation.[11] They merely fixed a once living tradition on paper so as to preserve it for all time.[12] Her studies attempt to recover the actual melodies of the Second Temple period, which she argues were faithfully represented in the Masoretic accentual system, which the Masoretes themselves only partially understood. Though they were aware of the fact that the system represented a rich musical heritage, they themselves were apparently not musicians as such. Consequently, they focused their attention primarily on the linguistic features of that system and used it to work out elaborate grammatical treatises on the accentual system they had inherited.

The studies in Deuteronomy, Song of Songs, and Nahum summarized here are much more modest in their intention than those of Haïk-Vantoura. My interest focusses on the rhythmic nature of specific ancient texts, as reflected in the distribution of disjunctive accents. Discernable rhythmic patterns are observed, both in terms of elaborate concentric structural design and the repetition of what appear to be repeated "metrical refrains." Though these refrains do not appear to reflect the repetition of identical melodic units in the sense of the repeated refrains or choruses in the hymnic tradition of Western Christianity, these structures do seem to reflect similar musical structures from a rhythmic perspective. I must defer to scholars with greater skills in the history and nature of music to explain in detail the full

---

11. S. Haïk-Vantoura, *La Musique de la Bible Révélée* (Paris: Dessain et Tolra, 1970): 67-71 and *passim*.

12. See Paul E. Kahle, *The Cairo Geniza*, 2nd ed. (New York: Frederick A. Praeger, 1959): 82-86 and 103. The word *te'amim*, according to Moses ben Asher, who took it from the "Elders of Bathyra" (sages living during the first century C.E.), had a wide range of meanings including: taste, intelligence, command, reason or cause, sense of meaning, accent or intonation. I am indebted to John Wheeler for this reference. Kahle was aware of the fact that the meaning of the verbal root behind this word includes to sound, resound, proclaim, or celebrate.

significance of these rhythmic structures, which emerged in studies of the Masoretic accentual system in specific biblical texts.

MASORETIC RUBRICS OF INDICATED ORIGIN
IN CODEX LENINGRAD (B19a)

Aron Dotan
Tel Aviv University

The value of the Leningrad Codex B19a (henceforth: L) as a primary source for the Ben-Asher school of vocalization and accentuation cannot be exaggerated. It is one of the best specimens of evidence for this school's practice, and it certainly is, in the present state of events, the only complete source of the whole Bible text according to that school. It is the only evidence of Aaron Ben Asher's readings in certain parts of the text, where the other prestigious Codices, like the Aleppo Codex (henceforth: A) and the London Codex Or. 4445 are failing. The Codex is invaluable also in another respect, namely, as a source of pre-masoretic or extra-masoretic information, which preceded the stage of masoretic normativization of voweling and accentuation. I have shown this on previous occasions of our IOMS meetings in what regards the use of the *ḥaṭef* signs[1] and the use of the geminative *dagesh*,[2] and I have shown it elsewhere in what regards the ancient stress position.[3] All these three aspects permitted us a new insight into the history of Hebrew pronunciation as well as into the evolution of Hebrew graphemics.

Today we will look into still another aspect of the Leningrad Codex, namely, the masoretic evidence transmitted by name. We hope to show the uniqueness and the invaluability of the Codex in this respect as well.

---

1. A. Dotan, "*Patḥé Ḥaṭfin* - A Study into the Evolution of the Tiberian Vocalization", *A. Even-Shoshan Jubilee Volume on the Occasion of his Seventieth Birthday* (Jerusalem 1983):157-165. [Hebrew]

2. A. Dotan, "Deviation in Gemination in the Tiberian Vocalization", *Estudios Masoreticos* (V Congreso de la IOMS), ed. E. Fernández Tejero (Madrid 1983):63-77.

3. A. Dotan, "Residues of an Ancient Penult Stress in the Tiberian Tradition", *Z. Ben-Ḥayyim Jubilee Volume on the Occasion of his Seventieth Birthday* (Jerusalem 1983):143-160. [Hebrew]

As is well known, the whole bulk of the Masora is an anonymous opus, put together generation after generation by a large number of masoretic scholars. They all contributed to the combined pool of masoretic information, reducing themselves and hiding behind the humble veil of anonymity. Only some isolated names of Masora scholars came down to us, very few of them from the direct evidence of masoretic notes. There are, indeed, some names enumerated in certain sources, as, for instance, the names of the ancient ones, אלקדמא, mentioned in the 'Treatise on the Shewa',[4] but within masoretic notes proper, their number is scarce. It is noteworthy to remark here that the Aleppo Codex has no mention of names whatsoever, not even of the Maʿarvaʾe or Madinḥaʾe schools.

There is of course the material gathered by Ginsburg in his voluminous compilation, where, in his first volume,[5] under חלופים he quotes a number of masoretic scholars. Thus he names רבינו גרשם מפריז (#643),[6] רב אידי (#647), ר׳ יוסף זרקא (#649), חזקיה הנקרן (#649), יעקב (#652), מרחא (#658), ר׳ מושי (#659), ר׳ משא (#662), רבי משה (#663), רב נחמן (#664), מר שמואל בר שילת בנהרדעא (#673), ר׳ פינחס (#669). Besides these he also quotes prestigious codices, like אל נגדאדי (#664), which should perhaps be בבלי (#646), and אל שרקי,אלבגדאדי (#645), ירושלמי (#654), the well known הללי (#648), also טבריה and מחזורא רבא ובעלי חמת (#650, 660), he quotes לונכרט (#655), סיני (#665), ספר עזרא (#667), which is mentioned already in the Talmud.[7] And of course reference to correct codices is very common in the terms of ספר מוגה (#657), ספר מדויק (#656), נסחא קשיטא (#671) (= the true version), and to ancient versions, as is קדמון (#672), these latter ones not referring to a definite text.

However, this collection of names is very unreliable. Ginsburg himself, in the fourth volume of his compilation[8] admits that: "As nearly every line of these ... Rubrics is taken from the Massorahs of a different MS. it is practically impossible to specify against the several lines the particular Codex to which the individual line belongs. I shall therefore simply state that I have compiled these Rubrics from the different MSS. which I have minutely described in my *Introduction to the Massoretico-Critical edition of the Hebrew Bible*, chap. XII, p. 469 &c."

---

4. K. Levy, *Zur masoretischen Grammatik* (Stuttgart 1936): ט-י.

5. C. D. Ginsburg, *The Massorah Compiled from Manuscripts*, vol. I (London 1880):604-612.

6. The numbers in brackets indicate Ginsburg's paragraph numbers.

7. Bavli, Moʿed Qaṭan 18b (Mishna), and see Rashi *ad locum*.

8. C. D. Ginsburg, *ibid.*, vol. IV (Vienna 1897-1905):422.

Since most of Ginsburg's manuscripts are relatively late, and mostly European, it is evident that the names he gathered are, to a large extent, of relatively late scholars and late Codices. Only few names seem ancient, as רב פינחס, a ninth century masorete,[9] and as מורא, also one of the early masoretes, and the Codex מחזורא רבא. These early names in later manuscripts are no evidence of ancient provenance, they were meant to add to the prestige of the Codex and of the scribe, but most of their readings do not seem reliable and genuine.

It is therefore important to find readings from ancient masoretes in an early source such as the Leningrad Codex, which, although copied in the year 1009 C.E., draws upon very early sources, as has been proven.[10]

It is perhaps worthwhile to mention, before we go into details, that the decisive part of the Masora notes of indicated origin in L are in the Hagiographa (כתובים). Out of dozens, only three are not from there -- two from the Pentateuch and one from the Prophets (Judges). This means that the scribe of L consulted additional sources only when he came to the Hagiographa, or that his *Vorlage(n)* were of such a kind that they contained only evidence in the Hagiographa. In any case, there certainly is a difference in the masoretic transmission of the two parts of the manuscript. This has to be borne in mind in further study of the Codex, but it should not affect our present study and conclusions.

The Masora of indicated origin in L may be divided into three main categories: 1) referring to specific masoretes or codices, 2) referring to a school or a tradition, 3) referring to a different reading (חילוף) without disclosing the name of the specific masorete or school.

To the first category belong some notes mentioning the names of רב פינחס[11] or רבי פינחס,[12] and of the Codex מחזורה רובה.[13] The three occurrences of ספר מוגה[14] seemingly do not involve one *definite* correct master text, but a group of reliable texts. This is clear in two of the occurrences which show an abbreviation of the plural: בסיפ׳ מוגה - the dot on the *he* suggesting the Aramaic reading - בסיפרין מוגהין or בסיפרי מוגהי. Incidentally, the message in two of the three notes is obscure.

---

9. As I have shown in *The Diqduqé Hatte'amim of Ahăron ben Mošé ben Ašér* (Jerusalem 1967), (henceforth: DQHT): 303-305.

10. See above notes 1-3.

11. Masora *magna* (Henceforth: MM) to Prov 20:11.

12. MM to Job 32:3.

13. MM to 2 Chron 2:5, Ps 109:16, Job 32:3, Prov 3:12.

14. Masora *parva* (henceforth: MP) to Eccles 7:23, Eccles 9:15, Lam 2:18.

The reference to readings of [אנשי טיב[ריה]¹⁵ and בעלי טבריה¹⁶ seem to mean a group of people having in common a local reading habit. The two terms are apparently synonymous, and בעל טבריה which is found once,¹⁷ refers not to a single Masorete but to the same group, the *yod* of בעלי having been erroneously omitted.

Anshé Ṭeverya or Baʿalé Ṭeverya, as holders of specific readings, may or may not be regarded as a 'school'. But Ben Asher and Ben Naftali, at this stage of transmission, should not be regarded as individuals, but definitely as two separate schools. This is evident also from the relative abundance of the notes mentioning their names. They belong therefore to the second category. To this category belong also the relatively numerous notes mentioning the Palestinian versus the Babylonian traditions -- חילופי מערבאי ומדינחאי.

In the third category there are notes introducing a variant reading through the abbreviated term מחלפ¹⁸ (=מחלפין), or even without such a term.¹⁹ In these cases the originator's name was omitted.

The masoretic information of the notes of the first and third categories is quite scarce, and their number practically negligible: of the first category there are just eight notes -- 5 Masora *magna*, 3 - *parva*; of the third category there are 15 notes - most of them (14) Masora *parva* and only 1 Masora *magna*. The third category can still be subdivided since at least eight of the fifteen חילופים can be traced to the Ben Asher/Ben Naphtali controversy, and should therefore be counted as part of the second category referring to a specific school.

We thus come to the main bulk of origin-indicated Masora in the Codex. The BA/BN group and the מערבאי/מדינחאי or west/east group. Our main concern is the contribution of the Codex in these two types of חילופים. The time will not permit us to go into details. It is also quite unnecessary after the illuminating study of Prof. Fernándo Díaz Esteban published about twenty years ago.²⁰ In this study Prof. Díaz Esteban also dealt with notes of the first category in as much as they concern BA/BN. Examining the material of the Masora *Magna* alone he showed there that the express BA/BN information in the Masora of that Codex is not always consistent

---

15. MM to 2 Chron 2:5.
16. MM to Job 32:3.
17. MM to Prov 3:12.
18. E.g. MP to 1 Chron 10:7, Dan 7:12.
19. E.g. MP to 1 Chron 27:1, 2 Chron 13:11.
20. F. Díaz Esteban, "References to Ben Asher and Ben Naftali in the *Massora Magna* Written in the Margins of MS Leningrad B19A", *Textus* 6 (1968):62-74.

with the evidence of Mishaʾel Ben ᶜUzziʾel in his *Kitab al-Khulaf* (henceforth: MbU).[21]

All that is left to me is to point out and evaluate those differences between BA/BN that are not recorded at all by Mishaʾel Ben ᶜUzziʾel. Of the BA/BN group there are 13 notes (9 Masora *Magna*, 4-*parva*) involving the readings of 21 words. Out of these 21 words not less than six are not mentioned at all in MbU. That is, a reliable source prior to Mishaʾel, who flourished at the earliest in the middle of the eleventh century,[22] testifies to almost 30 percent of variances not known to Mishaʾel. These variances are:

		BA	BN	
1)	MM Ps 31:12	וְלִשְׁכֵנַי	וְלִשְׁכֵנָי	(Shewa-Gaᶜya = full vowel)
2)	MM Ps 62:4	תְרָצְחוּ	תְּרָצְּחוּ	
3)	MM Ps 119:94	לְךָ־אֲנִי	לְךָ אֲנִי	
4)	MM Dan 4:27	בֱנִיתָה	בֱּנִיתָהּ	
5)	MP Dan 7:10	קרי רבבן	?	
6)	MP 1 Chron 12:7	[BA וִירִישִׁיהוּ]	וִישִׁיהוּ	

Four of these have supporting evidence. No. 3 is supported by a rule of *Diqduqé Ha-Ṭeᶜamim*, chapter 12; No. 2 is supported by David Qimḥi in his commentary *ad locum*. Nos. 1, 2, 3, 6 occur in that list of *hillufim* of BA/BN, which has been known prior to the Lipschütz publication of MbU from Geniza manuscripts (n. 21). This list, (henceforth: Hilist), found in many medieval Bible manuscripts, has been printed by Jacob Ben Ḥayyim at the end of his Second Rabbinic Bible (Venice 1524-5) (henceforth: V) and by Ginsburg.[23] Hilist has been rejected as absolutely unreliable.[24] It seems, now, that although erroneous, there is a nucleus of genuine old tradition in Hilist and it should be re-examined carefully.

Moreover, in four out of the remaining 15 words that do occur in MbU - Mishaʾel's evidence is not fully consistent with the evidence in the masoretic notes.

---

21. L. Lipschütz, "Mishael Ben Uzziel's Treatise on the Differences between Ben Asher and Ben Naphtali", *Textus* 2(1962): א-נה.

22. See L. Lipschütz, "Kitāb al-Khilaf - the Book of the Ḥillufim", *Textus* 4 (1964):1. And see, however, also, DQHT: 321 n. 6.

23. Op. cit. (note 5):571-591.

24. See, e.g., L. Lipschütz, op. cit. (note 21):4. The list of differences between BA and BN published by S. Baer in the Baer-Delitzsch Bible edition are valueless since they are mostly a fabrication to fit his theory of a correct text, see P. Kahle, *The Cairo Geniza*² (Oxford 1959):116.

			L	MbU
1)	MM	Ps 106:39	BA בְּמַעַלְלֵיהֶם	בְּמַעַלְלֵיהֶם
2)	MM[25]	Ps 116:17	BN לך אזבח	לְךָ־אֶזְבַּח (agreement)
3)	MM	Ezek 7:28	(BA הִטָּה־)[26] BN הִטָּה־	הִטָּה־ (agreement)
4)	MP	2 Chr 8:11	BA בָּאָה	בָאָה

So these four and the six new divergences mentioned above make together ten out of 21 words, namely, in almost fifty percent of the cases Misha'el's evidence is questioned by a source earlier than himself, a source the reliability of which we have no reason to question.

The contributions of the Leningrad Codex to the other group of this category, to the חילופי מערבאי ומדינחאי is relatively even greater.

There are 44 words to which there are 46 Masora notes - 19 Masora *magna*, 27 Masora *parva* (two words having two notes each, both Masora *magna* and *parva*). It is useful to compare these notes to the "regular" list of חילופי מערבאי ומדינחאי. By "regular" I mean the list printed by Jacob Ben Ḥayyim at the end of his Second Rabbinic Bible and by Ginsburg.[27] This list appears also in manuscripts, such as, for instance, in the Leningrad Codex itself, in its Masora *finalis*.[28] The various versions of this list are pretty much identical, with Ginsburg's list, being the latest compilation, a little more comprehensive. I also compared our material to the apparatus of Ginsburg's Bible edition,[29] where he cites specific readings of מערבאי or מדינחאי not found in the regular list but gathered by him from Masora notes in individual Bible manuscripts.

Comparison to the combined data of all these lists (henceforth: MaMad) shows that of the 44 west/east divergences of the Masora notes in L only 23 are found in MaMad (including Ginsburg's isolated readings in his Bible edition). Most of these notes are consistent with the evidence of MaMad. When the various versions of

---

25. MM to Ps 119:94.

26. Only the reading of BN is recorded in the MM. That of BA is here implied from L.

27. Op. cit. (note 5):591-599. See also his article "On the Relationship of the so-called Codex Babylonicus of A.D. 916 to the Eastern Recension of the Hebrew Text", *Recueil des travaux rédigés en mémoire du Jubilé Scientifique de Daniel Chwolson* (Berlin 1899):149-188.

28. Ginsburg published this list for the Prophets and Hagiographa in his article (note 27):152-165.

29. C. D. Ginsburg, *The Old Testament*, vols. 1-4 (London 1926).

with only one of the sources (list or isolated reading), I regarded it as an agreement, assuming that the Masora note confirms the evidence of one of the sources (lists, etc.) against the others. Only two out of the 23 are inconsistent with all the other sources - the MP notes to הַמְּלוּכָה (1 Chron 10:14) and to לְשָׂרֵינוּ (Dan 9:8) - and there is good reason to assume a scribal error on the part of the copyist of these notes in the Codex.

However, the remaining 21 divergences of L are not found in MaMad *at all*. This is completely new evidence of an Eastern reading. Some of these readings - four in all - could be corroborated by Babylonian manuscripts, such as the Berlin manuscript of the Hagiographa Or. 680,[30] the Codex Petropolitanus of the Prophets of 916 C.E.[31] and two manuscripts cited by Yeivin.[32] But most of it is completely new, new even compared to the list of divergences of the Masora *finalis* in that very same Codex L. The scribe of the Codex had a different source for his Masora notes, a source which held more information than the "regular" list (MaMad) which he copied in his Masora *finalis*. In other words, in his time there existed a tradition of west/east divergences which had not been codified in the "regular" list. The Masora of the Codex is an invaluable source for this tradition.

It is only proper to state in this context that residues of the Eastern tradition are imbedded in the text of the Leningrad Codex itself. It is well known, as attested by the scribe Samuel Ben Jacob, that the Codex has been changed to fit the Aaron Ben Asher school.[33] We have shown that the changes were not done on a common Tiberian text, but rather on a non-normative text, which carried some anomalies in matters of stress, gemination and *ḥaṭefs*.[34] Among the anomalies we can count also the adherence to some Eastern readings.

---

30. See the photographic reproduction of this manuscript, ed. I. Yeivin (Jerusalem 1983), where the text has the reading of what in L, MP to Dan 9:9, is attributed to the Easterns.

31. *Prophetarum Posteriorum Codex Babylonicus Petropolitanus*, ed. H. Strack (Petersburg, 1876). Here in Jer 25:27 we find the *ketiv* וקור (*qere* וקיר) attributed in L, MM to Neh 9:14 (s.v. ומצרות), to the Easterns.

32. I. Yeivin, *The Hebrew Language Tradition as Reflected in the Babylonian Vocalization* (Jerusalem, 1985):968, quotes a manuscript where the same *ketiv* זכר is attributed to the Easterns as in L, MM to Ezra 10:28; and on p. 1043 he quotes another manuscript which brings the same note regarding the Western reading (ל׳ למערב) as in L, MM to 2 Chron 33:6 (s.v. וידעוני).

33. See, e.g., F. Pérez Castro, "Corregido y correcto", *Sefarad* 15 (1955):27.

34. See above notes 1-3.

From among the 44 words where the Masora displays the Eastern tradition - in five instances the text of Leningrad agrees with it:

1. מַעֲשֵׂי (MM Ps 8:4) - למרנח מעשי אצבעתיך כח יו
למער כח ה
The common reading is with *he* מַעֲשֵׂה as in A, V, etc., and as in the regular lists of MaMad. It seems that A has been corrected from מעשי to מעשה).

2. אֵילִים (MP 1 Chron 29:21) - למער חס י קדמ. Indeed, the common Western reading is here אֵלִים. So A and V.

3. לְהָשִׁיב (MP 2 Chron 6:23) - ל חס למער. In L and A the spelling is *plene*, namely, the reading in both codices follows what this masoretic note considers מרינחאי. In V, however, it is defective לְהָשִׁב.

In addition to these clear-cut testimonies the evidence is not so clear in two other cases:

4. אֹמַר (MP Ps 50:12) ל מל למערב. Since L's spelling is defective its reading is מרינחאי. However, A, V, too, have it defective. Moreover, L was corrected from *plene* אוֹמַר to defective אֹמַר. It is hard to assume a correction from מרינחאי to מערבאי even in L.

5. בְּבֹאָם (MP 2 Chron 20:10) - למרנ חס. However, not only L but also A, V etc., spell it defective. It is even possible that there is a correction in A - from *plene* to defective.

It is not surprising that Codex Leningrad has Eastern readings. This is known especially from the composite words and proper names which are written as one word in one tradition, and in two words in the other, as for instance כְּמוֹ־קַד (Ps 102:4), and בַּל־אַמִּים, where all four occurrences[35] are written in L in two words as in the Babylonian tradition. But here we have readings, which one could have considered mistakes, had it not been for the Masora notes.

Surely, although the orthographic reliability of L suffers, once again we realize that the Codex reveals residues of ancient deviating traditions; here - ancient Eastern spellings that have not come down to us in other sources. In this respect, too, Codex Leningrad, precisely because of its deviating readings, which diminish the orthographic reliability, is an invaluable instrument to the study of the Masorah and to the understanding of its evolution.

---

35. Ps 44:15, 57:10, 108:4, 149:7.

HEBREW READING TRADITIONS OF THE JEWISH COMMUNITIES

Ilan Eldar
University of Haifa

Hebrew was uninterruptedly used as a spoken language from its earliest days until the first generations following the destruction of the Second Temple, probably till the end of the 2nd century AD.[1] Since Hebrew ceased serving as a living language until it was re-established as a commonly used vernacular at the end of the 19th century,[2] its history evolved in two different directions throughout all spheres of Jewish culture: as both a written language (at least by the intellectual elite), and also as a language of reading and prayer. This long span between the time when Hebrew was a living language and the time when it was revived is called the "intermediate period".[3] The subject of this paper is how knowledge of Hebrew reading was realized during this intermediate period.

I

The term "reading language" is applicable to the language of Jews who use Hebrew as their second (indirect) language, while one of the Jewish vernaculars serves as their first (direct) language. This term refers to the language of Hebrew liturgical texts,[4] or to texts bearing a religious significance, which Jews read out from a book in front of them or recite from memory. Reading of the Holy Scriptures or of prayers is not uniform among Jews: differences are noticeable in the phonetic values

---

1. As to when Hebrew ceased to be the spoken language of the Jews see Segal (1928): 12-15: Bendavid (1967): 153-165; Kutscher (1972): 57-60.
2. See Rabin: 47-54; Rabin (1985); Téné (1986): 151-155.
3. See Téné (1985): 145-150; a different attitude concerning the beginning of the intermediate period is presented in Morag (1985).
4. For the status and use of Hebrew as a liturgical language see Rabin (1969).

of the vowel signs and letters, and in the pronunciation of words and grammatical forms. Differences may be found between individuals (e.g., Jewish scholars and laymen) or between groups. The present study, however, is concerned with differences between the various Jewish communities rather than with individual differences, as the latter are not so prominent when compared with differences between one community and another.

The standard way of reading Hebrew texts in each community is based on an oral tradition, whereby phonological and morphological information is wholly or partially passed down orally from generation to generation, from father to son and from teachers to their pupils. The various Jewish traditions of reading Hebrew aloud are referred to as "reading traditions" or "traditional pronunciations".[5]

Reading of a liturgical Hebrew text by a Jew who does not speak Hebrew reflects, therefore, his command of the cut-and-dried system of the reading instructions (taught locally), interpreting the affinity between the phonology and morphology and the morphophonology of the language and the orthography of the text.

We can distinguish three kinds of Hebrew reading traditions of the main liturgical texts read by Jewish communities:

a. reading tradition of the Bible.

b. reading tradition of the Mishnah and the Hebrew portions of the Talmud.

c. reading tradition of the prayers and liturgical poetry (*piyyuṭim*) of the Holiday Prayer Books (*maḥzorim*).[6]

Reading of the Mishnah and the Talmud and of the Prayers and *piyyuṭim* are usually considered as one reading tradition, namely the reading tradition of postbiblical literature.

There is, however, a distinct difference between reciting the Bible and reciting the postbiblical literature (particularly the Mishnah), in that the former has a binding and commonly accepted vocalization and cantillation while the latter never received any systematic vocalization. Consequently reading traditions of the Bible by all Jewish communities (except the Samaritans) are fully documented in writing: the Biblical text together with its orthography, vocalization and cantillation signs, all fully authorized, comprises all the necessary phonological and musical units, and conveys all the information required for the identification of the grammatical forms and the metrical structure of the words. The reader's reliance on the oral tradition is

---

5. See Morag (1969): 128-131; Morag (1971): 1121.

6. See Eldar (1978), introduction: 14-15; Eldar (1980): 81-83; Kutscher (1972): 17; Morag (1985): 15-17; Sharvit (1988): 71-72.

therefore reduced to the realization (by sounds and melodies) of the graphic signs. On the other hand, reading traditions of postbiblical literature have only partial graphemic representation (as does the Samaritan reading tradition of the Bible). Since the postbiblical texts are transmitted from generation to to generation without vocalization, their orthography reveals only part of the vowel system, although they abound in vowel letters relative to the biblical text. Consequently, this orthography reveals the vocalic and metrical structure of the words only partially, and the reader himself must therefore supply what is unspecified in the text he is reading according to the commonly accepted oral tradition of his community.[7]

Regarding the differences between the reading tradition of biblical and postbiblical literature, Jewish communities (except the Samaritans) accepted the Tiberian system as the only authoritative vocalization (and cantillation) of the Bible, so that they all read from the same vocalized (and cantillated) biblical text. The differences between the reading traditions of the communities are, therefore, only differences between various pronunciations.[8]

On the other hand, the different ways of reading post-biblical literature, for which obligatory vocalization was not adopted, are not only differences between pronunciation values of the written symbols, but also, and mainly, differences as to the forms of the words.[9]

Students of Hebrew generally accept that quite a few unique phonological and morphological features of the reading traditions of the Mishna, (as well as of the Biblical tradition of the Samaritans) can be traced to ancient times, and that they may well represent dialectic differences of the early postbiblical period (i.e., up to the intermediate stage).[10]

Having no way of determining geographical differences in living Hebrew in ancient times on a regional basis, students of Hebrew must confine themselves to drawing isoglosses along the time axis. It is commonly agreed that the Jewish traditions of reading the Mishnah (and the Samaritan traditions of reading the Bible) reflect various kinds of Hebrew used in the Land of Israel by the last generations of Hebrew speakers.[11]

---

7. See Morag (1969): 132; Morag (1988) :42-45.
8. See Téné (1985): 112.
9. See Morag (1971): 1121-1122.
10. See Morag (1986); For an attempt to discuss the relationship of reading traditions to dialects and the transformation of dialects into reading traditions see Morag (1969a).
11. See Ben-Ḥayyim (1957), introduction: 12; Ben-Ḥayyim (1977): 1-2. 252-253; Morag (1969): 133-135.

The dialectological dimension of Hebrew used as a liturgical language[12] transmitted orally is represented not only by living oral traditions kept alive by the Jewish communities, but also by "living" written traditions, that is, the orthography and vocalization of ancient and excellent manuscripts of Tannaitic literature, mainly the Mishnah.[13]

A recent study of the different traditions of Mishnaic Hebrew[14] has shown that the one reflected in ancient manuscripts which only contain the Mishnah (i.e., without the Talmud) represent the Palestinian type of Mishnaic Hebrew. This tradition comprises two different reading traditions of the same Mishnaic text: A Western one transmitted in manuscripts of Italian provenance (e.g., Codex Kaufmann and Codex Parma A), and an Eastern one transmitted in manuscripts of Eastern origin (e.g., Codex Parma B, Geniza fragments with Babylonian vocalization). According to the author of this study, Prof. Moshe Bar-Asher, both reading traditions crystallized in the Land of Israel; later, one tradition went west through one school of learning, and the other went east through another. Many of the elements distinguishing the two traditions, as well as most of their common elements, were traced back to Mishnaic language prevalent in the Land of Israel, whose various dialects differed from each other to a greater or lesser extent. It is very likely therefore, that these two traditions in the Land of Israel reflect two dialects spoken here; but since data on local variation in Hebrew during the period of the Second Temple is lacking, it is impossible, of course, to determine the geographical distribution of these features in the two dialects.[15]

II

There are several important points to be mentioned about the divergence of the reading traditions, including their classification into groups and their genetic affinity

---

12. The term "liturgical" is used "to include not only the language of the prayer books, but also the language of those parts of the postbiblical literature which were regarded as significant parts of the religious heritage, mainly the Mishna and Talmud" (Morag [1969]: 141, n.31).

13. See Eldar (1980): 78-81.

14. Bar-Asher (1984).

15. Bar-Asher (1984): 209, 214-215, 217; cf. Bar-Asher (1988): 16-19.

to the ancient reading traditions as reflected in the different Hebrew vocalization systems, generated in the 7th and 8th centuries A. D.[16]

The musicologist Avraham Zvi Idelsohn, who at the beginning of the century recorded the biblical reading of the communities in Jerusalem synagogues[17] tried to group these reading traditions. He described nine pronunciation types, which reflect the geographical diversification of Hebrew pronunciation at the end of the intermediate period. He divided them into two main groups according to the pronunciation of the vowels.[18] One group comprises five types: The Samaritan, the Sephardic (residents of Arabic-speaking countries - Syria and Egypt; residents of Greece and Turkey as well as the Slavic countries in the Balkan Peninsula), the Moroccan (all of North Africa), the Babylonian (Iraqi Jews), and the Portuguese (descendants of Portuguese Marranos in the cities of Western Europe) and Italian Jews. The second group comprises the following types: Yemenite, Persian, Ashkenazic (German, Polish and Russian Jews) and Daghestani.

Another two-way division is into Ashkenazic and Sephardic, in accordance with the classical split of the Diaspora since the beginning of the Middle Ages into two main blocs: Sephardic Jewry and Ashkenazic Jewry.[19] Yet, since not all the traditions of the dispersed Jewish communities are accurately accounted for in this two-way division into Ashkenazic and Sephardic traditions, a trilateral division was introduced and accepted, which reflects the uniqueness of the Yemenite tradition as well.[20]

A group unto itself, apart from the three-way division into Sepharic, Ashkenazic and Yemenite, is the Samaritan tradition.[21] This divergence from the mainstream is due to the fact that Jews read the Bible according to its Tiberian vocalization, whereas the Samaritan reading tradition of the Pentateuch (similar to the various

---

16. For the question of dating for the vocalization systems see Chomsky (1941/2); M. Weinreich (1964): 142; Morag (1968): 840-841; Chiesa (1979); Dotan (1981).

17. Idelsohn (1913); Idelsohn (1913a); See Morag (1986a); Téné (1986): 144-146.

18. See Idelsohn (1913): 42, 140. Cf. Morag (1986a): 166-168; Téné (1986): 144-146.

19. The distinguished Yiddish scholar Max Weinreich maintains such a division. See M. Weinreich (1964): 139, 240-241.

20. See Morag (1963): 287-290; Morag (1971): 1130.

21. See Ben-Ḥayyim (1977): 2-3 , 256; Morag (1983), introduction, 13; Morag (1971): 1122.

reading traditions of the Mishnah in all Jewish communities) is not based on a vocalized text, and is transmitted orally in the community from generation to generation, as the Samaritans did not work out a binding vocalization system.[22] The Samaritan tradition has a historical explanation as well, since the Samaritans were not exiled and their spiritual center has always been within the boundaries of the Land of Israel, in Shechem (Nablus), that is, around Mount Gerizim.

As to the historical roots of the three-way division: It is commonly accepted that the differences between the vowel system of the Yemenite, Sephardic and Ashkenazic pronunciations are traceable to the reading traditions reflected in the Hebrew vocalization systems[23] prevailing in the great Jewish centers of Western Asia (the Land of Israel and Babylonia) during the Gaonic period.[24]

A comparative study leads to the following conclusions regarding the relationship of the current traditions to the various systems of Hebrew vocalization.[25]

a. The Sephardic pronunciation tradition - maintained by the Eastern communities (except Yemen); North African communities and the Sepharid communities of Europe - is a direct derivative of the Palestinian pronunciation tradition (five vowels),[26] which underlies the two vocalization systems, the one called the "Palestinian"[27] and the other called the "Palestinian-Tiberian".[28] Apparently the "Palestinian" pronunciation was transmitted in the Middle Ages from the Land of Israel through Italy to Spain and was disseminated by the Jews exiled from Spain to the countries of their dispersion.[29]

---

22. See Ben-Ḥayyim (1977): 4-7.

23. For an analysis of the principles upon which the Hebrew vocalization systems are based see Morag (1962) :17-44, 65-67, 69-74.

24. H. Yalon was the first to recognize that there are many points of agreement between the current traditional pronuciations of the main Jewish communities and the reading traditions reflected in the vocalization systems. See Morag (1970).

25. The subsequent presentation summarizes an article (in Hebrew) by the present writer (see Eldar, 1989). See also the discussion of this question in Klar (1951); Morag (1963): 287-292; Morag (1971): 1122-1129.

26. See Morag (1980): 142.

27. For a classification of Hebrew biblical and non-biblical texts with Palestinian vocalization see Revell (1970); Dotan (1971): 1433-1427 and Yahalom (1988).

28. The Palestinian-Tiberian system is also called "Fuller-Palestinian" (Morag), "Enlarged Tiberian" (Yeivin), "Tiberian non-conventaional" (Dotan). For a general survey of this vocalization system see Morag (1968); Dotan (1971): 1461-1466; Eldar (1978): 180-184 (and the literature cited there), 212 (index).

29. See Morag (1985a): 31 ; Morag (1986): 749.

b. The Yemenite pronunciation tradition continues the pronunciation underlying the Babylonian vocalization (six vowels),[30] which at the end of the Gaonic period made its way to Yemen and has been preserved by the Yemenite Jews up to the present.[31]

c. The current Ashkenazic pronunciation (of Central and Eastern European Jews), which makes a phonemic distinction between all seven vowels of the Tiberian vocalization, (*qamaṣ, pataḥ, ṣere, segol, ḥolam, šuruq/qubuṣ, ḥiriq*) can be traced back to the middle of the 14th century. Before then (since the Jews resettled in Germany at the beginning of the 10th century), the Palestinian pronunciation tradition (of 5 vowels: a, e, u, o, i) has been used by the Ashkenazic Jews.[32] It turns out that the adoption of a different pronunciation by the Ashkenazic communities of the Middle Ages is the result of certain phonological developments in the vowel system that were taking place in their (Jewish) spoken language, i.e., Yiddish (including its Hebrew-Aramaic component).[33] The new qualitative distinctions /a~o‖u/ /e~ey‖ay/ which arose in their spoken language as a result of phonetic shifts a>o‖u, e>ey‖ay,[34] were transferred to the reading language of the sacred texts (i.e., Hebrew) in accordance with the standards of traditional Tiberian vocalization (i.e., distinctions between *qameṣ* and *pataḥ* on the one hand, and between *ṣere* and *segol* on the other).[35]

It is worth noting that a change in pronunciation took place in medieval Spain as well. Prof. Sh. Morag has recently cited several examples (from transcriptions of Hebrew words in Roman letters contained in a Hebrew-Latin glossary) indicating that Babylonian pronunciation features existed in the Hebrew tradition of Jewish communities in Spain. On the basis of this evidence he conjectured that before the

---

30. A detailed treatment of the Babylonian vocalization is presented in Yeivin (1985).

31. For the relation between the Yemenite communities and Gaonic Babylonia see Morag (1963), introduction: 16-17; M. Weinreich (1964): 234-327; Morag (1988): 45-46.

32. Concerning the Palestinian pronunciation the Ashkenazic communities had before the 14th century see M. Weinreich (1964): 240-246; Eldar (1978), introduction: 19-20 (and the articles of H. Yalon cited there); Morag (1985a): 30-31.

33. For the origin of Yiddish and the origin of the Semitic (Hebrew-Aramaic) component in Yiddish see M. Weinreich (1954); Katz (1985). For the geography of the Hebrew component in Yiddish see U. Weinreich (1965): 12-28.

34. See M. Weinreich (1980): 456-457, 627, 671, 688-689 (for a>o), 475-6, 613, 685, 689-690 (for e>ey).

35. See Eldar (1986): 77-79.

Palestinian pronunciation tradition was transplanted from Italy to Spain and adopted by Spanish Jewry, some communities may have used the Babylonian pronunciation for a certain period, apparently till the middle of the 10th century.[36] Morag singles out a phonological factor - the disappearance of the distinction between *qamaṣ* (*gadol*) and *pataḥ* in the vowel system of Babylonian pronunciation - as the factor which obliterated a characteristic feature of this tradition and facilitated the acceptance of the Palestinian tradition by the Spanish communities whose pronunciation tradition was originally Babylonian. He also points out the workings of historical and sociolinguistic factors that were instrumental in bringing about the decline and fall of the Babylonian pronunciation tradition in medieval Spain on the one hand, while consolidating the status of the Palestinian tradition there on the other.[37]

III

The fact that the Ashkenazic community developed, under the influence of its vernacular, phonemic realizations between Tiberian *qamaṣ* and *pataḥ* on the one hand and between Tiberian *ṣere* and *segol* on the other shows that in a bilingual situation where a non-spoken liturgical language and a spoken language co-occur throughout a Jewish community, the main factor influencing change in the oral reading tradition of the liturgical language (i.e., Hebrew) is the (non-Hebrew) vernacular. The nature and extent of this influence depend on sociocultural circumstances and, especially, on the relations between the sound systems of the two languages. It should be noted, of course, that a difference must be made between blurring or reinterpretation of distinctive features in the language tradition as a result of the influence of the vernacular and a complete substitution of the liturgical pronunciation tradition by another tradition as caused by sociohistorical factors (as happened in medieval Spain, according to Prof. Morag).

The phonological system of the vernacular may influence that of the orally transmitted language tradition[38] under two main conditions:

---

36. The linguistic evidence available for the assumption that the Babylonian tradition was transplanted from Babylonia into medieval Spain is fully examined in Morag (1980) :151-152; Morag (1986): 750-754.

37. For the linguistic and sociolinguistic factors that might have played a role in the process of establishing the Palestinian pronunciation in Spain see Morag (1980) :152-156; Morag (1986) :755-757.

38. An attempt to formulate patterns of interference see Morag (1963): 275-281; see also Ben-Ḥayyim (1957), introduction: 20-23.

(1) The vernacular does not make all the distinctions (phonemic and allophonic) made by the liturgical language (more precisely: the distinctions expressed by the graphemes - including the vocalization signs - of the liturgical language). This relation between the sound systems of the two languages may result in the fading and obliteration of certain distinctions or in the merging of two phonemes which are phonetically close in the pronunciation tradition of the liturgical language.

As examples let us take four features of the Ashkenazic pronunciation: the realization of ע and א as zero and of the soft ח as ט; the realization of a double (geminate) consonant as a simple one; and the merger of שׂ and ס ,שׁ (in some varieties).³⁹

(2) There are distinctions in the vernacular which exist in the liturgical language too, but they are realized differently. Here, certain distinctions in the liturgical language ceased to be made in their original form and the external manner of distinction is adopted in the Hebrew language tradition of the community as a substitution for the original distinctions. In any case, the adoption of the new manner of realization to the pronunciation system of Hebrew does not affect the phonemic relations in this language.

As an example of reinterpretation of distinctive features let us consider one peculiar feature of the Yemenite Hebrew tradition: in Sanʿa and in Central Yemen, undageshed ג is pronounced as an affricate [ǧ] and the dageshed ג is pronounced as a velar aspirated stop. This distinction corresponds to the one found in local Jewish Yemenite Arabic.⁴⁰

Such manifestations of adoption to the phonetics of the vernacular are also detectable when new phonetic developments occur in the vernacular. This, for example, is how the above-mentioned development of the diphthongal pronunciation of the Ṣere in Ashkenazic Hebrew can be explained.

During the Old Yiddish Age (1250-1500) a diphthongal pronunciation of long (closed) [e] (originally long [e] or lengthened short [e] in an open syllable) began to take root in Yiddish. When the dialectal map of Yiddish in Europe was taking shape⁴¹ the pronunciation of the diphthongized [e] split geographically: [ei] in South-Eastern and North-Eastern Yiddish and [ai] in Southern-Central Yiddish. The phoneme /ei|ai/ spread from the German component of Yiddish - in which the shift

---

39. See U. Weinreich (1965): 7.
40. See Morag (1963): 25-28.
41. For a skeletal outline of the dialectal groupings of Yiddish see Jaffe (1954): 102-107; see also U. Weinreich (1965): 19-20.

ē > ei‖ai began - to the Hebrew component as a reflection of *ṣere* (in an open syllable) as in: *eyme* (אֵימָה) *breyshis* (בְּרֵאשִׁית) and *meyle* (מֵילָא), and as a reflection of *segol* (in an open syllable) in a small group of words where Yiddish-speakers pronounce them as *ṣere*, as in: *meylekh* (מֶלֶךְ) and *keyver* (קֶבֶר). In a closed syllable, the short (closed) [e] of Earliest Yiddish (corresponding to stressed short [e] of Middle High German) is not lengthened, and is pronounced as non-diphthongized [e] in all varieties of Yiddish. The contrast between a closed syllable and an open syllable is therefore the source of vocalic differences in the Yiddish words corresponding to the Hebrew pairs: שֵׁד־שֵׁדִים, מֵת־מֵתִים etc. In the singular the syllable ends in a consonant, and the realization of the vowel marked by the *ṣere* is [e] in all dialects (*shed, met*), whereas in the plural the stressed syllable (in Yiddish) ends in a vowel, and the *ṣere* is therefore represented in the Hebrew component by /ei‖ai/ (*sheydim shaydim*), etc.[42]

As for the liturgical Hebrew of Ashkenazic Jews (starting from the second half of the 14th century), the significance of the shift e > ei ai taking place in their vernacular can be summed up in the formula: "*ṣere alef* = [ei]". When reading of the Bible and reciting the prayers and *piyyuṭim* were linked to texts with Tiberian vocalization (which distinguishes between *ṣere* and *segol*), Ashkenazic readers began realizing the graphic distinctions according to the vocal distinctions which had taken root in the vowel system of the vernacular and sustained themselves in words of Hebrew-Aramaic origin. This is how the diphthongal realization of the *ṣere* was clearly distinguishable from the monophthongal realization of the *segol*. The innovation *ṣere* - [ei] or [ai] (depending on the Yiddish dialect, since the regional differences in the Ashkenazic Hebrew correspond to those of Yiddish) entered, then, Ashkenazic Hebrew due to the Hebrew component of Yiddish, but in the liturgical reading (and in any case, in the correct reading) this innovation was subjected to the rules of Hebrew grammar reflected in the Tiberian (Masoretic) pointing.[43]

IV

The use of a non-Hebrew vernacular (i.e., Jewish language) by Jewish speakers and its influence on their liturgical language (i.e., Hebrew) caused by the diglossic (bi-lingual) situation lead us to the more general problem of how the reading traditions of Jewish communities crystalized.

---

42. See note 34.
43. See note 35.

In a recent study on the historical unity of Hebrew,[44] Prof. David Téné expresses a new view about the factors influencing the formation and emergence of various pronunciation traditions of Hebrew: the most important factor was the linguistic milieu of the users of Hebrew in the "intermediate period". During this long period, which lasted for nearly 1700 years, Hebrew was everywhere a second language, whereas the first language was one of the Jewish vernaculars. As a result Hebrew pronunciation was realized only through intentional learning of reading, which was possible only by a process of diaphonic identification. The users of Hebrew identified the phonetic values represented in the graphic signs with phonetic values found in the Jewish vernaculars that have always accompanied the knowledge of Hebrew language.

Thus the main factor in the formation of various pronunciations in the reading of the Bible and in crystalization of reading traditions among Hebrew-users in the various communities is interlingual identification; consequently, it is unlikely that phonetic properties that do not conform to the phonetics of Jewish vernaculars will be found in the Hebrew reading traditions.[45]

The actual facts are much more complex and while this is not the place to sort out the details, it should be pointed out that even among Yiddish-speaking Jews, where the pronunciation of the liturgical language and the phonetics of the vernacular are conceived as two contiguous systems, no total identity can be found.[46] In Yemen too, the resistance of the Hebrew tradition is obvious: the traditional Yemenite pronunciation of the vowels, which is traceable to the Babylonian Hebrew tradition of the Gaonic period, has not surrendered to the influence of the vernacular. As we compare the relation between the vowel phonemes of the liturgical language and those of the Jewish Yemenite Arabic, we see that the liturgical language preserves two contrasts that do not exist in the vowel system of the vernacular: [e~ö] on the one hand (realizations of *ṣere* and *ḥolam*) and [å~a] (realizations of *qamaṣ* and *pataḥ*) on the other.[47]

Knowing how Hebrew was traditionally learned by all Jewish communities in a much more formal and conscious manner than the vernacular,[48] we are hardly surprised that the relationship between the phonetics of the vernacular and the rules for reading Hebrew is not universally automatic, and the influence of the vernacular

---

44. Téné (1985).
45. Téné (1985): 111-114.
46. See M. Weinreich (1964): 135-137; U. Weinreich (1965): 8-9.
47. See Morag (1963): 278.
48. See U. Weinreich (1965): 8; Morag (1969): 137-138.

could be checked by adherence to tradition and by the requirement of a precise formal transmission of the sacred text (particularly insistance on accurate realization of the vowel signs). It seems that the information gleaned from the various phases of development of the reading tradition in fact confirms Prof. Max Weinreich's position in his study of the beginning of Ashkenazic pronunciation: "Only the naïve believe that reading of the Scriptures by each and every community is ingrained with the mark of its vernacular."[49]

It appears that the widely held view[50] still explains satisfactorily the crystallization of Hebrew oral language traditions in all Jewish communities: Hebrew traditional pronunciation wherever accompanied by a spoken Jewish language is a product of earlier Hebrew reading practices and the effects of the phonemic system of the Jewish vernacular.

Needless to say, external influence is not the only factor in shaping the oral language tradition; autonomous innovations caused by any internal process of analogy and hypercorrection or by normative aspirations should also be considered.

V

The fact that neither oral tradition has been static since Hebrew was frozen as a liturgical language (serving for the reading of the Bible and postbiblical literature) is of primary importance for assessing the historical value of the linguistic information conveyed by the oral tradition. Such a historical evaluation depends on our ability to recognize and investigate the information that the oral tradition preserved from the Hebrew language before the latter ceased to be spoken; and it is also based on our ability to deduce from the present form of the oral tradition all the influences resulting from the contact of the liturgical language with the vernacular of the community along the chain of transmission, as well as intra-Hebrew innovations resulting from other factors.[51]

It goes without saying that only a comprehensive diachronic investigation of each pronunciation tradition would provide us the data necessary for a proper knowledge of the original linguistic (in this case: the phonological) information that

---

49. M. Weinreich (1964): 136.

50. See, for example, Idelsohn (1913a): 536; Morag (1963): 269; M. Weinreich (1964): 135-137.

51. The question of evaluating historically a reading tradition and the necessary conditions for a reconstruction of a past stage in the history of a reading tradition to be considered valid are discussed in Morag (1969): 133, 140-146.

constituted the reading tradition (i.e., the oldest form of the language that the oral tradition reflects).

The penultimate stress, which is common to the present-day pronunciations of Samaritans and Yemenite and Ashkenazic Jews, is an interesting example of how reconstruction of past stages from present day similarities must proceed very cautiously.

A suggestion that the place of stress in pronunciations of those communities was a survival of an old Hebrew penult (thus continuing a common origin) was first put forward by Idelsohn[52] and fifteen years later was accepted by M. Z. Segal (in his pioneer work on Hebrew phonetics). Segal writes:[53]

"The agreement among the three dialects - the Ashkenazic, the Yemenite and the Samaritan - which are so remote from one another geographically, and among which there must have been no contact or mutual influence ever since the destruction of the Second Temple, in itself provides the proof that the penult accentuation common to all of them must have derived from Old Hebrew itself ... which generally had penultimate stress."

In the light of recent studies on the origins of the penultimate stress in each of the three traditions mentioned we can no longer accept the Idelsohn-Segal hypothesis. The main conclusions of these studies are as follows (detailed evidence and actual proof are not specified here).

(a) There is sufficient evidence for considering the Samaritan penult accentuation as secondary, being the result of retraction of the stress from the final to the penultimate syllable, which was taking place while Hebrew was still a spoken language. Since the previous stress position in Samaritan Hebrew corresponds to the Tiberian tradition, it is inconceivable that the present-day Samaritan stress system is a direct continuation of the penult stress of Proto-Hebrew or of a Hebrew dialect with the ancient penult accentuation.[54]

(b) As for the stress system of Yemenite Hebrew, first it should be noted that a comparison of Yemenite Hebrew with Tiberian Hebrew shows that there is no regular penultimate stress but rather a tendency towards it in certain circumstances but not in others. It should also be noted that the number of penultimate stresses in reading the Mishnah is much higher than in reading the Bible. In view of the close affinity between the Yemenite reading tradition of the Mishnah and the tradition of

---

52. Idelsohn (1913).
53. Segal (1928): 75.
54. See Ben-Ḥayyim (1963): 152. A full description of stress in the Samaritan tradition is given by Ben-Ḥayyim (1977): 48-52.

Babylonian Jews in the Gaonic period, it might be assumed that regarding the rules of penultimate stress the traditional reading of Yemenite Jews continues and preserves the Babylonian tradition. On the one hand this assumption has no foundation, since what is known about the stress patterns in Babylonian texts of the Mishnah is rather scanty; on the other, it has no support, since the stress of biblical Hebrew in Babylonian texts corresponds with the Tiberian stress.[55] The affinity of the vernacular of the Yemenite Jews in this respect is much more obvious. A comparative study of the stress of the Hebrew reading and the Jewish Arabic dialects they use reveals several features of similarity and correspondence, indicating that the penultimate tendency in the Yemenite reading is very likely an outcome of the influence of the vernacular on the reading of both the Bible and the Mishnah.[56]

(c) As for the Ashkenazic stress system, general penultimate stress in Ashkenazic Hebrew, coupled with blurring of the ultimate unstressed vowel,[57] is a relatively recent and extraneous phenomenon. A variety of evidence indicates that during the early days of the Ashkenazic tradition (the "pre-Ashkenazic" reading tradition), the stress patterns were not different from the traditional Tiberian stress of ultimate and penultimate stress.[58] It is quite likely that the shift towards penultimate stress (and in a limited number of cases toward an antepenultimate stress) was a local development of the German-origin pattern of root-initial stress on Yiddish words of Hebrew origin.[59]

To sum up: the present-day approximate similarity between Samaritan, Yemenite and Ashkenazic stress should not be considered evidence of a common origin (i.e., ancient non-Tiberian tradition) where penult stress prevailed (or which was more penultimate than the Tiberian tradition). Contrary to what Idelsohn, Segal and others thought, the penult stress of these three communities is not primary: the place of stress in their present-day reading is a result of later developments under the influence of the vernacular on the traditional pronunciation of Hebrew (the case of Yemenite and Ashkenazic Hebrew) on the one hand, and a result of a process (the retraction from ultimate towards penultimate) that took place in Hebrew itself (the case of Samaritan Hebrew) on the other.

---

55. See Yeivin (1985): 243.
56. See Morag (1963): 229, 246, 259-260.
57. See U. Weinreich (1965): 43.
58. See Eldar (1978): 170.
59. See Leible (1965).

Literature Cited

Bar-Asher, M. (1984)
מ' בר-אשר, "הטיפוסים השונים של לשון המשנה", תרביץ נג [תשמ"ד]: 187-220.

Bendavid, A. (1967)
א' בנדוד, לשון מקרא ולשון חכמים, תל אביב תשכ"ז.

Ben-Ḥayyim, Z. (1957)
ז' בן חיים עברית וארמית נוסח שומרון, כרך ראשון: מבוא - כתבי הדקדוק, ירושלם חשי"ז

Ben-Ḥayyim, Z. (1963)
- "בדבר מקוריותה של הטעמת מלעיל בעברית", ספר חנוך ילון [עורכים ש' ליברמן ואחרים], ירושלים תשכ"ג, 150-160.

Ben-Ḥayyim, Z. (1977)
- עברית וארמית נוסח שומרון, כרך חמישי: לשון תורה, ירושלים תשל"ז.

Chiesa, B. (1979) *The Emergence of Hebrew Biblical Pointing - The Indirect Sources*, Frankfurt am Main.

Chomsky, W. (1941/2) "The History of our Vowel System in Hebrew", JQR XXXII:26-49.

Dotan, A. (1971) "Masorah", *Encyclopaedia Judaica*, vol. 16, Jerusalem: 1401-1482.

Dotan, A. (1981) "The Relative Chronology of Hebrew Vocalization and Accentuation", PAAJR XLVIII:89-92.

Dotan, A. (1983)
א' דותן, "שקיעי הטעמת מלעיל עתיקה במסורת הטברנית", מחקרי לשון מוגשים לזאב בן-חיים [עורכים מ' בר-אשר ואחרים], ירושלים תשמ"ג: 143-160.

Eldar, I. (1978)
א' אלדר, מסורת הקריאה הקדם-אשכנזית, מהותה והיסודות המשותפים לה ולמסורת ספרד, כרך א: ענייני הגייה וניקוד, ירושלים תשל״ט.

Eldar, I. (1980)
- ״מסורות הקריאה ומחקר המבנה התנועי של צורות לשון חכמים״, קובץ מאמרים בלשון חז״ל, ב, ירושלים תש״ם: 78-83.

Eldar, I. (1985)
- ״מסורות ההגייה של העברית״, מסורות, כרך ג-ד [עורך מ' בר-אשר], ירושלם תשמ״ט: 3-36.

Eldar, I. (1986)
- ״ניקודו של מחזור וורמייזא״, מחזור ווֹרמייזא כ״י בית הספרים הלאומי והאוניברסיטאי, כרך המבואות [עורך מ' בית אריה], ירושלים תשמ״ו: עה-צט.

Idelsohn, A. Z. (1913)
א״צ אידלזון, ״ההברה העברית״, השילוח כח [תרע״ג]: 34-42, 132-141.

Idelsohn, A. Z. (1913a) "Die gegenwärtige Aussprache des Hebräischen bei Juden und Samaritanern", MGWJ:525-545, 697-721.

Joffe, J. A. (1954) "Dating the Origin of Yiddish Dialects" *The Field of Yiddish*, Vol. I (ed. U. Weinreich), New York:102-121.

Katz, D. (1985) "Hebrew, Aramaic and the Rise of Yiddish", *Readings in the Sociology of Jewish Languages*, (ed. J. Fishman), Leiden:85-103.

Klar, B. (1951)
ב' קלאר, ״לתולדות המבטא העברי בימי הביניים״, לשוננו יז [תשי״א]: 72-75.

Kutscher, E. Y. (1972)
י' קוטשר, ״מבעיות המילונות של לשון חז״ל, ערכי המילון החדש לספרות חז״ל [עורך י' קוטשר], רמת גן תשל״ב: 29-82.

Leibel, D. (1965) "On Ashkenazic Stress", *The Field of Yiddish*, Vol. II (ed. U. Weinreich), The Hague:63-72.

Morag, S. (1962) *The Vocalization Systems of Arabic, Hebrew, and Aramaic*, The Hague.

Morag, S. (1963)
ש׳ מורג, העברית שבפי יהודי תימן, ירושלים תשכ״ג.

Morag, S. (1968)
- ״ניקוד״, אנציקלופדיה מקראית, כרך ה, ירושלים תשכ״ח 837-857.

Morag, S. (1969) "Oral Traditions as a Source of Linguistic Information", *Substance and Structure of Language* (ed. J. Puhvel), Berkeley and Los Angeles:127-146.

Morag, S. (1969a) "Oral Traditions and Dialects", *Proceedings of the International Conference on Semitic Studies*, Jerusalem: 180-189.

Morag, S. (1970)
ש׳ מורג, ״על חנוך ילון ודרכו בחקר הלשון״, מולד כו [תש״ל]: 297-302.

Morag, S. (1971) "Pronunciations of Hebrew", *Encyclopaedia Judaica*, vol. 13:1120-1145.

Morag, S. (1980)
ש׳ מורג, ״בין מזרח למערב: לפרשת מסירתה של העברית בימי-הביניים״, דברי הקונגרס העולמי השישי למדעי היהדות, כרך ד, ירושלים תש״ם:141-156.

Morag, S. (1983) "The Yemenite Tradition of the Bible: The Transition Period", *Estudios masoreticos (V Congreso de la IOMS) dedicados a H. M. Orlinsky* (ed. E. Fernández Tejero), Madrid. 137-149.

Morag, S. (1985)
ש׳ מורג, ״העברית כלשון עילית של תרבות - תהליכי גיבוש

ומסירה בימי-הביניים בארצות הים התיכון״, פעמים 23
[תשמ״ה]:9-21.

Morag, S. (1985a)
- "העברית בארצות הים התיכון: מסירתה במשך הדורות״, כנס
פריז - דברי הכנס העברי המרעי החמישי באירופה של ברית
עברית עולמית, ירושלים תשמ״ה:29-36.

Morag, S. (1986) "The Pronunciation of Hebrew in Medieval Spain", *Salvacion en la palabra, Homenaje al Alexandro Díez Macho*, Madrid:749-758.

Morag, S. (1986a)
ש' מורג, "אברהם צבי אידלסון ומחקר מבטאיה של העברית״,
יובל [קובץ מחקרים של המרכז לחקר המוסיקה היהודית],
כרך ה: ספר א״צ אידלסון, ירושלם תשמ״ו, קס-קסח.

Morag, S. (1986b) "De la tradition au dialecte: Problèmes d'enquête linguistique", *Massorot - Studies in Language Traditions and Jewish Languages*, vol. II (ed. M. Bar-Asher and S. Morag), Jerusalem:103-112.

Morag, S. (1988)
ש' מורג, "לשון חז״ל - העדויות שבעל-פה: מהותן והערכתן״,
דברי הקונגרס העולמי התשיעי למרעי היהדות, ישיבות מרכזיות:
הלשון העברית והארמית, ירושלים תשמ״ח:39-54.

Rabin, Ch, (-)
ח' רבין, עיקרי תולדות הלשון העברית, ירושלים [חסרה שנת
דפוס].

Rabin, Ch. (1969) "Liturgy and Language in Judaism" *Language in Religious Practice* (ed. W. J. Samarin), Massachusetts:131-155.

Rabin, Ch. (1985)
ח' רבין, "לשון המקרא ולשון חכמים בעברית בת זמננו״, מחקרים
בלשון, כרך א [עורך מ' בר-אשר], ירושלים תשמ״ה, 273-285.

Revell, E. J. (1970) *Hebrew Texts with Palestinian Vocalization*, Toronto.

Sarvit, Sh. (1988)
ש' שרביט, "מחקר לשון חז"ל - הישגים וצרכים", דברי הקונגרס העולמי התשיעי למדעי היהדות, ישיבות מרכזיות: הלשון העברית והארמית, ירושלים תשמ"ח:61-73.

Segal, M. Z. (1928)
מ"צ סגל, יסודי הפוניטיקה העברית, ירושלים תרפ"ח.

Téné, D. (1985)
ד' טנא, "לענייו אחדותה ההיסטורית של העברית וחלוקתה לתקופות", מחקרים בלשון, כרך א [עורך מ' בר-אשר] ירושלים תשמ"ה:101-551.

Téné, D. (1986) "La pronociation traditionelle de l'hébreu et l'émergence de l'hébreu parlé de nos jours", *Massorot*, vol. II, (ed. M. Bar-Asher and S. Morag), Jerusalem, 139-158.

Weinreich, M. (1954) "Prehistory and Early History of Yiddish: Facts and Conceptual Framework", *The Field of Yiddish*, vol. I (ed. U. Weinreich), New York:73-101.

Weinreich, M. (1964)
מ' ויינרייך, "ראשית ההברה האשכנזית בזיקתה לבעיות קרובות של היידיש ושל העברית האשכנזית", לשוננו כז-כח [תשכ"ד]:131-147, 230-251, 318-339.

Weinreich, M. (1980) *History of the Yiddish Language*, Chicago.

Weinreich, U. (1965)
א' ויינרייך, "העברית האשכנזית והעברית שביידיש - בחינתן הגיאוגרפית", ירושלים תשכ"ה [נדפס לראשונה ב"לשוננו" כרך כד:242-252 ; כרך כה:57-80, 180-196]

Yahalom, J. (1988)
י' יהלום, "הניקוד הארצישראלי - המחקר והישגיו", לשוננו נב [תשמ"ח]:112-143

Yeivin, I. (1985)
ר׳ ייבין, מסורת הלשון העברית המשתקפת בניקוד הבבלי, א-ב, ירושלים תשמ״ה.

BENEDICTI ARIAE MONTANI ... DE MAZZORETH RATIONE ATQVE VSV

Emilia Fernández-Tejero
Instituto de Filología, CSIC - Madrid

"Cognovimus (Montanum) pium, doctum ac prudentem";[1] "è di gran dottrina et qualità rarissima";[2] "je me sens attiré, contraint et volontairement ravi et transporté a aimer et revérer le dit Signeur Arias Montanus et ce comme personage que sans envie ni afection je apercoy a la verité etre autant bien doué et rempli de graces divines que j'en cognoisse";[3] "las cosas que concurrieron en este doctor son estas: La primera ser muy buen letrado y gran teólogo y muy visto en todo género de ciencias y lenguas ... Su trato y su conversación eran de un santo; su humildad sobrepujaba a la de todos cuantos le quisiesen bien y le amasen";[4] "small of stature and certainly not robust, witty and charming in conversation, he combined the directness of the scholar with a singular gentleness and attraction".[5]

These could have been the words of a Roman, French, Spanish or English woman in love; but, in fact, they are the words of serious intellectuals: Pope Gregory XIII, Cardinal Sirleto, the printer Plantin, Fray Juan de San Jerónimo and the British Hispanist A. F. G. Bell.

Benito Arias Montano was born in Fregenal de la Sierra, in the diocese of Badajoz (Spain), in 1527; he studied at the universities of Sevilla and Alcalá de Henares, professed in the Order of Santiago, took part in the Council of Trent, was the chaplain of Philip II and collected manuscripts and books for the library of El

---

1. D. Ramos Frechilla, "La políglota de Arias Montano", *Revista Española de Estudios Bíblicos* III (1928): 52.
2. T. González Carvajal, *Elogio histórico del Doctor Benito Arias Montano*, "Memorias de la Real Academia de la Historia", vol. VII: 166.
3. D. Ramos Frechilla, "La políglota", p. 38.
4. F. Pérez Castro y L. Voet, *La Biblia Políglota de Amberes*, Madrid 1973 :33.
5. A. F. G. Bell, *Benito Arias Montano*, Oxford 1922: 54.

Escorial, where he was the first librarian; he took an active part in the politics of his time, as a counselor of the Duke of Alba (the Governor of the Netherlands), and travelled to Portugal, sent by the Spanish King, for an almost secret mission; in 1592 he retired to the convent of Santiago, Sevilla, where he was elected prior; he died on July 6, 1598.

Arias Montano wrote prose and poetry; in prose, commentaries to the books of the Old and New Testament, works on theology, philosophy, philology, geography, archaeology, numismatics, chronology and criticism; he translated the commentary of D. Kimhi on Isaiah, Jeremiah and Malachi from Hebrew into Romance and Latin, and the *Itinerario* of Benjamín de Tudela, into Latin; in Latin verse, he composed didactic and lyric works, translations of the Psalms; in Spanish, he wrote some sonnets and a paraphrase of the Song of Songs.[6]

The most interesting epoch of his life was undoubtedly the period between 1568 and 1572 when, by an express wish of Philip II, he directed the edition of the so-called *Arias Montano's Polyglot*, *Plantiniana* or *Antwerp Polyglot* (after the name of the printer or the place where it was printed) or *Biblia Regia* [*Royal Bible*] (after its sponsor).

The initial idea of this edition arose in the mind of the printer Plantin who, in the beginning, just tried to reprint the *Complutensian Polyglot*, published between 1514 and 1517, under Cardinal Ximenez de Cisneros' patronage. Some of the six hundred copies of this work were lost in a shipwreck on their way to Italy; the extant copies were being sold beyond price and Plantin erroneously thought he was doing the business of his life. But the money Philip II had lent in advance had to be paid back with copies of the Bible; the cost was at Plantin's expense and Arias Montano himself wrote to Zayas, secretary of the king, saying that "Plantin only earned with the edition the service he did to God and the king and the profit for the Christian community".[7] In compensation, Plantin was named "Royal Prototypographer".

The most personal collaboration of Arias Montano to the Polyglot was perhaps the composition of the Treatises that constitute volume VIII, namely the *Apparatus*, with its various contents: *Comvnes et familares hebraicae linguae idiotismi, Liber Joseph, sive de arcano Sermone, Liber Ieremaie, sive de Actione, Thvbal-Cain, sive de mensvris sacris, Chanaan, sive de duodecim gentibus* ... and, among them, *Benedicti Ariae Montani Hispalensis de varia in hebraicis libris lectione ac de Mazzoreth ratione atqve vsv:* eight pages composed of a *Praefatio ad lectorem, Benedicti Ariae Montani*

---

6. Cf. L. Morales Oliver, "Avance para una bibliografía de obras impresas de Arias Montano", *Revista del Centro de Estudios Extremeños* II (1928): 171-236.

7. D. Ramos Frechilla, "La políglota", p. 43.

de Psalterii Anglicani exemplari animadversio (rejecting the value of a Hebrew codex of this Psalter against bishop Gugliemus Lindanus' opinion) and a list of four pages, with the headline קָרִי & יַתִּיר & כְּתִיב.
Leaving aside the pages devoted to the Psalter, which deserve a special study, I will focus on the *Praefatio ad lectorem* and the list.

But let us first remember what the status of the Spanish exegesis in the 16th century was. Broadly speaking, we can perceive the existence of two streams or tendencies, not totally antagonistic, but opposite enough to provoke inflamed quarrels. On the one hand, the humanists, longing for the original linguistic sources, grammarians, defenders of the literal meaning (at least on the first step of interpretation), to whom the Old Versions were but a secondary tool of research, as was the case with Gaspar de Grajal, Martín Martínez de Cantalapiedra, Luis de León and Benito Arias Montano. On the other hand, the scholastics, more traditional, to whom the Vulgata was incorrupt, perfect and divinely infallible, partisans of the Versions, not very much inclined towards grammar, members of the so-called 'party of Jesus Christ', who labelled the partisans of the biblical text in its original language as Judaizers or Hebraizers, as was the case with Bartolomé de Medina and León de Castro.

But, on this occasion, we are not faced with another case of typical Spanish behaviour. According to Luther, "if the opinion (of the Rabbis) does not agree with all the Scripture, as the Rabbis with their glosses have gravely deformed all the Scripture ..., we simply reject that opinion".[8] As for Erasmus, "there were two principles fundamental to sound biblical exegesis ... that the grammatical sense must be interpreted by the highest linguistic skills, and that the spiritual sense ... must be expounded in close relationship to this grammatical sense". Münster showed in his edition of the Bible (1535) his knowledge of the rabbinical commentators; Vatablus and Sanctes Pagninus were accused of being Judaizers; Castellio said in the *Annotationes* to his Latin version of 1551, that "he confined himself to elucidating what the words plainly state", a statement that provoked Theodor Beza's strong criticism; Hunnius vigorously attacked Calvin in his *Calvinus Judaizans*, because Calvin had dared to say that *Elohim*, though a plural, did not refer to the Persons of the Holy Trinity, etc.

Unfortunately we have to agree with Basil Hall that "It would not be too great an exaggeration to say that the theological preoccupations and inhibitions among

---

8. D. Barthélemy, *Critique textuelle de l'Ancient Testament*, Fribourg/Göttingen 1982: *5.

both Catholics and Protestants prevented much real advance in higher or lower criticism until the eighteenth and nineteenth centuries".[9]

The accusation of Judaizers and Hebraizers easily reached the minds and pens of the theological adversaries; but matters could grow worse. The above mentioned Grajal, Cantalapiedra and Luis de León were imprisoned by the Holy Office. Arias Montano himself was criticized, accused, and persecuted, and even though it is not sure that any legal action was ever undertaken, he had to stay abroad while his friends were in prison.

The strongest criticism against *Arias Montano's Polyglot* was uttered by the redoubtable Professor of Greek at Salamanca, León de Castro, to whom "any scholar who went behind the Vulgata and consulted the Hebrew original deserved (as Castro himself knew little Hebrew) to be persecuted and condemned".[10] He accused Arias Montano of having used Sanctes Pagninus' Latin translation, based on the Hebrew text and different from Jerome's Vulgata; of having included in the *Biblia Regia* some *Apparatus* taken from the Rabbis, "irreconcilable enemies of our religion";[11] and in November 1576 he wrote a letter to the licenciate Hernando de Vega, counselor of the Inquisition, giving in detail all his objections and concluding: "Be it only for the sake of His Majesty's honor it ought to be prevented that a king as Catholic as Don Felipe ... suffers that those Bibles that seem to be the flag of the Synagogue are called *Filipinas* and *Royal Bible*".[12]

There were also many difficulties in achieving the pope's approval; in Rome, it was alleged, among other things, that the treatise *De Sermone arcano* could be cabbalistic, and that the *Talmud* was often quoted. Only Arias Montano's patience and charm could obtain the confidence of Pope Gregory XIII.

The charge of having substituted the rabbinic tradition as well as the pagan tradition of Erasmianism for the patristic one, almost caused the *Biblia Regia* to be entered into the *Index* of Maestro del Sacro Palacio (1607)[13] and the *Expurgatory Index* of 1612.[14]

---

9. B. Hall, *Biblical Scholarship: Editions and Commentaries*. "The Cambridge History of the Bible" III, Cambridge 1963: 82, 87 and 47.

10. A. F. G. Bell, *Benito Arias Montano*, p. 24.

11. J. Luján García, "Benito Arias Montano, datos biográficos", *Revista Española de Estudios Bíblicos* III (1928): 16.

12. P. J. Conde, "Arias Montano y la cuestión bíblica de su tiempo", *Revista del Centro de Estudios Extremeños* II (1928): 438.

13. *Ib.*, p. 467.

14. *Ib.*, pp. 449-450.

* * *

Let us return to the *Praefatio* to know the fundamental ideas exposed in it by Arias Montano:

- from the earliest times the Israelites maintained the reading of the Holy Books scrupulously.

- all measures were taken to avoid the smallest change both in the words and in the smallest trifle of the text.

- so, not only the truth of the books could be maintained uncorrupt, but the highest benefit of their wisdom was conserved.

- that treasure was called מָסֹרֶת, namely tradition or traditional, because it faithfully transmitted the variant readings of the Hebrew books, and was kept with such diligence, care and application that it prevented the tiniest discrepancies from sliding into the different copies and it avoided that these copies could be modified by the criteria of anyone.

- the slanderers who claim that the text was corrupted by the Jews, had to take into consideration that variant readings can only be found (apart from some clerical errors) in the related vowels or in some consonants with similar pronunciation or shape.

- there are also some odd examples, when two words, different in pronunciation and meaning, are written one in the text and one in the margin.

- these words, by tradition, or for any other reason, were kept with such veneration, that they deserved to be included in the *Mazzoreth*.

- the similarity and constancy of these *Mazzoreth* show the manifest help of divine Providence, because such a phenomenon does not occur in Chaldaic, Greek and Latin books.

- the *Mazzoreth* was born almost at the same time as the vicissitudes of the early Israelites.

- from the beginning, the words יתיר, קרי, כתיב, were used in the *Mazzoreth* to indicate variant readings, and this is their meaning: כְּתִיב, means that it is written thus in the text; קְרִי means that this was the way it was customary read; יַתִּיר teaches that there is a superfluous letter or point, contrary to the grammatical rule.

- the great calamity [that is the corruption of the text] claimed by those who ignore this very old *Mazzoreth* and who attribute this misfortune to Jewish envy (but they don't mention the author, the epoch and the reason why the Jews did it) has never existed.

* * *

And finally, the list: four pages, each of them with five columns, running from right to left, but bound in the Latin way; each column is arranged in two parts: the right one contains the *qerê*, and the left one, the *ketîb*.

The order of the books is the order shown by the Vulgata, namely Ruth, after Judges; Chronicles, Ezra and Nehemia, after Kings, followed by Esther, Job, Psalms, Proverbs, Ecclesiastes, Song of Songs, Isaiah, Jeremiah, Lamentations, Ezekiel and the Twelve Prophets (Daniel is missing). The number of the corresponding chapters and verses is indicated, and only a few errors of identification can be detected.

Occasionally a Latin note is added: *cum defectu*, if a letter is missing; *deficientia*, for a *ḥaser* reading; *abundat* or *redundat* for *yattîr*; *scribitur sed non legitur*, *legitur sed non scribitur*; *scribitur vna dictio, sed leguntur duae, scribuntur duae dictiones, sed legitur una*, literal translations of masoretic formulae.

The list contains almost a thousand items. As a sample, I collated the twenty-seven items corresponding to the Minor Prophets with the corresponding passages in the *Biblia Rabbinica* of Ben Ḥayyim and codex 118-Z-42 (M1) of Madrid University Library. The agreement with Ben Ḥayyim is total; as for codex M1, in two cases this codex keeps the *ketîb*, without masoretic note, and in two other cases there is a slight graphic difference in the *ketîb* or in the *qerê*.

And if you wonder why I chose the *Biblia Rabbinica* of Ben Ḥayyim and codex M1 for my collations, the answer is with Kipling: "that is another story".

MASORAH FIGURATA IN THE MIKDASHYAH:
The Messianic Solomonic Temple in a 14th-Century Spanish Hebrew Bible Manuscript

Joseph Gutmann
Wayne State University

Profiat Duran (1360-1412), the Spanish Jewish grammarian and polemicist, was convinced that the preservation and study of the text of the Hebrew Bible would assure his fellow Jews not only survival in this world, but eternal life in the world to come.[1] In biblical times, he contended, the sacrificial service in the Temple had effected forgiveness of sins, while in the present exile it was concentration on the Bible that atoned for sins. Just as the Temple in Jerusalem had been the abode of the Divine Glory, so the medieval Bible was the depository of Divine Law. The Bible was to the Spanish Jew a *mikdash me'aṭ*, a temporary substitute, during his exile, for the destroyed ancient Temple Sanctuary. Furthermore, Duran maintained, the Bible was divided into three parts, thereby corresponding to the tripartite division of the Solomonic Temple. "In view of [the many affinities between Holy Scriptures and the Sanctuary]," he wrote, "it was a felicitous idea on the part of those who named this great Book *mikdashyah* (the Sanctuary of God) for it is truly a Sanctuary of the Lord established by His own hands (cf. Exod 15:17). Indeed they call it *mikdashyah* [Sanctuary of God's abbreviated name, and not *mikdashyahweh* [Sanctuary of God's complete name] in order to indicate that [the Bible] is regarded only as a Sanctuary in the present exile -- at a time when the Divine Name and the Divine Throne are incomplete".[2] In his own lifetime, Duran lamented that Bible study was sadly

---

1. *Ma'aseh Efod*, 10.
2. *Ibid.*, 11-12. Cf. J. C. May, "The Morgan Library Hebrew Bible: Documents, Codicology, and Art History," *Studies in Bibliography and Booklore*, 16 (1986) :13-35; J. Gutmann, "*Masorah Figurata*: The Origins and Development of a Jewish Art Form," *Estudios masoreticos*, ed., E. Fernández Tejero (Madrid, 1983):59, n.18. Although a similar analogy for Scripture is used by Moshe ben Asher, it clearly refers to the biblical *'ohel mo'ed* and not to the rabbinic messianic Solomonic Temple. The words

neglected in favor of the study of Talmud, philosophy and Kabbalah, with disastrous results. Just as the Divine wrath was unsheathed against the Israelite nation in biblical times, for "they also shut the doors of the porch [of the Temple] and put out the lights; they did not offer incense and did not make burnt offerings in the Holy Place to the God of Israel [2 Chron 29:7] so [he felt, the Divine retribution visited upon Spanish Jewry in 1391] was due to the closing of the doors of the sacred Book [the Bible or *mikdashyah*] which is a Sanctuary established by His own hands, and to the extinguishing of its light".[3]

That the Bible was important to Spanish Jewry, as indicated by Profiat Duran, can be seen in the unique frontispieces to Spanish Hebrew Bibles, dating from the late 13th to the 15th centuries.[4] Primarily stemming from Catalonia, the frontispieces of some 25 surviving Spanish Hebrew Bibles (see figs. 1-2, following p. 77), often feature the splendid vessels of Solomon's Temple, which according to rabbinic tradition, were hidden away for the faithful.[5] At times, these frontispieces also

---

בבית קרש הקדשים are from 2 Chron 3:10; והקדש comes from Exod 26:33 and רחצר אהל מועד is taken from Lev 6:9, 19.

3. *Maʿaseh Efod*, 13-14.

4. The earliest Bible manuscript of this genre is dated Sunday, May 10, 1299, and comes from Perpignan, Kingdom of Majorca, cf. J. Gutmann, *Hebrew Manuscript Painting* (New York, 1978): 50-53. The Temple implements on two folios in a Hebrew Bible, dated Toledo, 1277, were probably painted on those folios at a later period, cf. Gutmann, "Messianic Temple": 138-39, n.8.

5. J. Gutmann, "Return in Mercy to Zion: A Messianic Dream in Jewish Art," in *Land of Israel: Jewish Perspectives*, ed. L. Hoffman (Notre Dame, 1986):235. The following additions and corrections should be made to *ibid.*, p. 252, n.3: J. Gutmann, "The Messianic Temple in Spanish Medieval Hebrew Manuscripts," in *The Temple of Solomon: Archaeological Fact and Mediaeval Tradition in Christian, Islamic and Jewish Art* (Missoula, Mont., 1976): 137 (13) should read: Written by Ḥayyim ben Saul Migdoli, called Vital Satori [M. Beit Arié and C. Sirat, *Manuscrits médiévaux en caractères hébraïques (Bibliothèques de France et d'Israel*, Jerusalem-Paris, 1979), II: 45]; Gutmann, "Messianic Temple":138 (16), should read: Formerly Sassoon Collection, Sotheby Auction, Nov. 21, 1978, lot 8.

It should be pointed out that Gutmann, "Messianic Temple": 135 (5 and 6) have identical inscriptions; 134-35 (1 and 3) have closely related inscriptions. Also 136 (11) and Gutmann "Return in Mercy": 252, n.3 (Gottheil No. 17) have similar inscriptions.

In addition, in Gutmann, "Messianic Temple," four manuscripts have inscriptions that are not related to the objects depicted -- 134 (2), 137 (12, 14) and 138 (18). These objects may have been added later, cf. Gutmann, 138-39 on (2) and 137 (12 and 14). In

prominently feature the Mount of Olives amidst the Sanctuary vessels since the messianic future will see the righteous dead rolling through underground caverns to emerge from the cleft Mount of Olives on the day of Resurrection.[6] From that vantage point, the resurrected righteous Jews will be able to view the restored objects of the Third Temple -- the rebuilt messianic Solomonic Temple. At that time, according to Maimonides, King Messiah will establish his kingdom and "all Israel will gather around him".[7]

---

the latter, the objects are painted over the inscriptions. Cf. T. Metzger, "Les objets du culte, le Sanctuaire du Desert et le Temple de Jerusalem, dans les bibles hébraïques médiévales enluminées, en Orient et en Espagne," *Bulletin of the John Rylands Library*, 53 (1970): 197, 199; B. Narkiss, *Illuminated Hebrew Manuscripts in the British Isles* (Oxford, 1982), I: 112.

Seven manuscripts [Gutmann, "Messianic Temple": 134-38 (1, 3, 11, 13, 18) and "Return in Mercy":252, n.3 ("Foa Bible" and Cairo Pentateuch)] all have an inscription from Numbers 8:4. It should also be noted that seven manuscripts are all related, and should be dated to the second quarter of the 14th century ["Messianic Temple": 136 (7-11) and "Return in Mercy": 252, n.3 (Cairo Pentateuch and Masson, MS 4)]. One of the seven manuscripts, 136 (7), is precisely dated *Shevat* (January or February) 1336.

To "Messianic Temple": 139, n.9 add: Kimḥi Commentary to 2 Chron 3:10 and Babylonian Talmud, *Baba Batra* 99a for cherubim with faces of children, and Babylonian Talmud, *Ḥagigah* 13b for cherubim with the face of a man. Page 140, n.12 should read: Treatise I, Chap. 3.14; n.13 add: Babylonian Talmud, *Menaḥot* 29a, *Tamid* 30b and n.15 add: Babylonian Talmud, *Menaḥot* 94b. To n.16 add: Rashi to Exod 25:31 and Babylonian Talmud, *Menaḥot* 28a-b; n.17 add: Rashi to Num 8:2; to p. 138, n.7 add: Gutmann, "Return in Mercy": 252, n.3 Cairo Bible has 3 folios and "Foa Bible" has 4 folios.

Cf. Narkiss, *Illuminated Hebrew Manuscripts*:102-4 for a description of the implements and No. 8, pp. 39-41 and No. 52, pp. 164-66 for two additional Spanish Hebrew Bibles with illustrations of the Temple vessels.

6. Gutmann, "Return in Mercy":236-37. On p. 253, n.7 add: M. Idel, "Prophetic Kabbala and the Land of Israel," in *Vision and Conflict in the Holy Land*, ed. R. I. Cohen (Jerusalem-New York, 1985): 114-15; Babylonian Talmud, *Ketubbot* 111a; H. C. Cavallin, "Leben nach dem Tode im Spätjudentum", *Aufstieg und Niedergang der römischen Welt*, ed. W. Haase (Berlin, 1979), Vol. 19.1: 319, n.557.

7. *The Code of Maimonides. Book Fourteen. The Book of Judges.* trans. A. M. Hershman (New Haven, 1949), Chapter XII.2: 241.

Thus, the frontispieces in the *mikdashyah* (or *mikdashiyah*) -- a Spanish Jewish visual metaphor for the hoped for messianic Temple in Jerusalem -- also served as a visible reminder of the promised salvation in the world to come. When the Spanish Jew read and studied his *mikdashyah*, he was sheltering himself, as it were, in a surrogate sanctuary while eagerly anticipating the permanent one to be established in the messianic future.

One of the most unusual depictions in a *mikdashyah* (Rome, Communità Israelitica, No. 19) shows the Temple vessels shaped by Hebrew micrography using words and phrases from the *masorah magna* to various books of the Bible, all of them allusions to the Temple implements.[8] Although dated Barcelona, Spain, 1325, the illustrations on the two folios were probably added later in the fourteenth century. In the first place, the Hebrew verses in large square Sephardi script framing the vessels have no relation whatsoever to the Temple objects, as was customary in most of the contemporary Spanish Hebrew Bible manuscripts. These unrelated verses on folios 214v and 216 (figs. 3-4) -- originally these folios were at the beginning of the Bible -- come from the books of Job and Proverbs. In the second place, folio 214 (fig. 5) shows clearly how the micrographic design was drawn over the square Sephardi letters, indicating a later addition. While most of the vessels reveal familiar shapes encountered in contemporary Hebrew Bible manuscripts, shapes such as the *mizbaḥ, shofar, zinzenet haman, shulḥan* and *leḥem hapanim*, the *menorah* and its branches differ and the insertion of the harp (*kinnor*) is a novel element. Only in one other Spanish Hebrew Bible manuscript (Private collection of the Sassoon family, Farḥi Bible, MS 368, p. 186 (fig. 6), dated 1366-82) do we find depictions of the musical instruments of the Temple. Of course, the inclusion of the *kinnor* was intended to recall the ancient Temple, in which the sacrifices were accompanied by the song and music of the Levites.[9]

---

8. I am greatly indebted to Rabbi Milton Weinberg for his gracious help with the *masorah magna*.

9. Gutmann, "Messianic Temple": 143, n.26. Cf. the vessels shaped by Hebrew micrography in a 14th-century Spanish *maḥzor*, fols. 11v-12, L. Avrin, *Micrography as Art* (Jerusalem, 1981), pl. 38 and Sotheby's Parke Bernet, New York, *Highly Important Hebrew Books and Manuscripts, Auction Catalog* (June 26, 1984), No. 47. Here, however, the micrography comes from the book of Psalms. I am indebted to Leila Avrin for this information. Cf. also pls. 37a-b and the discussion of the 1325 *mikdashyah* in Metzger "Les objets du culte": 182-84 and 187. For a description of the musical instruments in the Farḥi Bible, see *ibid.*, 191.

The custom in medieval Europe of shaping the *masorah magna* into figures, objects and designs may have been introduced by the Karaites in Abbasid Iraq in the eigth century -- our earliest evidence for this practice, however, comes only from late ninth-century Tiberias in Islamic Palestine.[10]

Amazing recent finds in Yemen have added a new dimension to the Spanish *mikdashyah* frontispieces. It appears that Qurʾan manuscripts from eighth-century Umayyad Yemen had frontispieces of images of an ideal mosque.[11] It is highly probable that the placement of the ideal mosque as frontispieces in large Qurʾan manuscripts may have influenced a similar practice of placing an ideal image of the Sanctuary and its vessels in Hebrew Bible manuscripts. We know that illustrated *ketubbot* existed in 11th-12th-century Islamic Egypt. These, too, were adaptations of contemporary illustrated Islamic marriage contracts.[12] I would suggest that decorating Spanish *ketubbot* in 13th-15th-century Christian Spain may simply be a continuation of a Jewish practice found in Fatimid Egypt. This custom may have been transmitted to the Jewish communities of Christian Spain via the Jewish centers of Islamic Spain. We know that, when the Jewish centers of Islam declined in the East, they began to flourish in the West, in southern Spain, although no material evidence has come to the fore to substantiate the conjecture that Jewish communities in Islamic Spain were the artistic bridge (for such practices as illustrated *ketubbot*, for

---

10. Gutmann, "Masorah Figurata":50-51. Whether the use of micrography for writing the *masorah magna* in shapes decorative, but difficult to read, is a uniquely Jewish art form, or is borrowed from Byzantine or Umayyad-Abbasid practices deserves an in-depth study.

The following corrections and additions should be made to *ibid.*: p. 54, and fig. 2 should read 15th century (cf. T. Metzger, "Ornamental Micrography in Medieval Hebrew Manuscripts," *Bibliotheca Orientalis*, 43 [1986]: 381-82); p. 60, n.26 add: Pentateuch [Leningrad Public Library, MS II.17], dated November, 13, 929, which was masorated by Ephraim ben Buyaʿa [B. Narkiss, *Hebrew Illuminated Manuscripts* (Jerusalem, 1984): 69--in Hebrew]; p. 61, n.27: The 1264 Bible (fig. 3) is in the private collection of A. Friedberg, Toronto, Canada. The 1480 Spanish Bible is from Seville [cf. T. Metzger, "Les manuscrits hébreux décorés à Lisbonne dans les dernières décennies du XVe siècle," *L'humanisme portugais et l'Europe* (Paris, 1984): 779].

11. H.-C. Graf von Bothmer, "Architekturbilder im Koran: Eine Prachthandschrift der Umayyadenzeit aus dem Yemen"; *Pantheon*, 45 (1987): 4-20.

12. J. Gutmann, "Jewish Marriage Customs in Art: Creativity and Adaptation," in *The Jewish Family: Metaphor and Memory* (New York, 1988): 61, nn. 21-22.

instance) linking Jewish communities in Islamic Egypt to Jewish communities in Christian Spain. Similarly, I would argue that the idea of placing frontispieces of ideal images of a mosque in Umayyad Qurʾan manuscripts may have influenced contemporary Jews to introduce an image of an ideal Sanctuary and its implements into Hebrew Bible manuscripts. The only indisputable evidence we have, however, are the 13th-15th-century *mikdashyah* manuscripts from Christian Spain.[13] Possibly, Umayyad Qurʾan and Hebrew Bible manuscripts traveled West to the new Umayyad centers of Spain, where they may have influenced the Jewish Bible tradition which took shape in Christian Spain. At this stage of our knowledge, such an hypothesis is tantalizing, but has little to support it.[14]

In conclusion: the Temple vessels we saw in a unique fourteenth-century Catalan Hebrew Bible manuscript, shaped by micrographic Hebrew letters taken from the *masorah magna*, are part of a Spanish Jewish tradition dating from the late thirteenth to the fifteenth century. The Bible, called *mikdashyah* (or *mikdashiyah*), was to the Spanish Jew a surrogate or temporary sanctuary. Reading and studying from his *mikdashyah*, he believed, would assure him salvation in the world to come, where he would behold the long-awaited rebuilt messianic Temple of Solomon with all its splendid vessels. The practice of placing an ideal Sanctuary with its vessels as frontispieces to Spanish Hebrew Bibles may have been influenced by earlier Islamic practices of placing an ideal mosque with its vessels as frontispieces to Qurʾan manuscripts.

---

13. Whether depictions of the Tabernacle and its vessels in two Islamic Hebrew Bible manuscript fragments from the tenth century represent such ideal Sanctuary images is difficult to determine. Cf. Gutmann, "Messianic Temple": 125 and 133, n.3.

14. My thanks to Prof. Stanley F. Chyet for his welcome comments and suggestions.

ILLUSTRATIONS

Figs. 1-2. Messianic Temple Vessels. Pentateuch. Istanbul, Karaite Synagogue in Hasköy, fols. 3v-4, Catalonia, second quarter of the 14th century. Courtesy of Mr. Albert Sonsino.

Figs. 3-4. Messianic Temple Vessels. Pentateuch. Rome, Communità Israelitica, No. 19, fols. 214v, 216, Catalonia, 14th century (the ms. itself was written in Barcelona in 1325). Courtesy of Dr. Luisa Mortara Ottolenghi.

Fig. 5. Masoretic Micrography with Verses from Prov. 3:18 and Job 28:15, 17 in frame. Pentateuch, Rome, Communità Israelitica, No. 19, fol. 214. Catalonia, 14th century. Courtesy of Dr. Luisa Mortara Ottolenghi.

Fig. 6. Musical Instruments of the Messianic Temple. Farḥi Bible. Jerusalem, Private collection of the late Rabbi S. D. Sassoon, No. 368, p. 186, Catalonia, 1366-1382. Courtesy of the late Rabbi S. D. Sassoon.

Figure 1

Figure 2

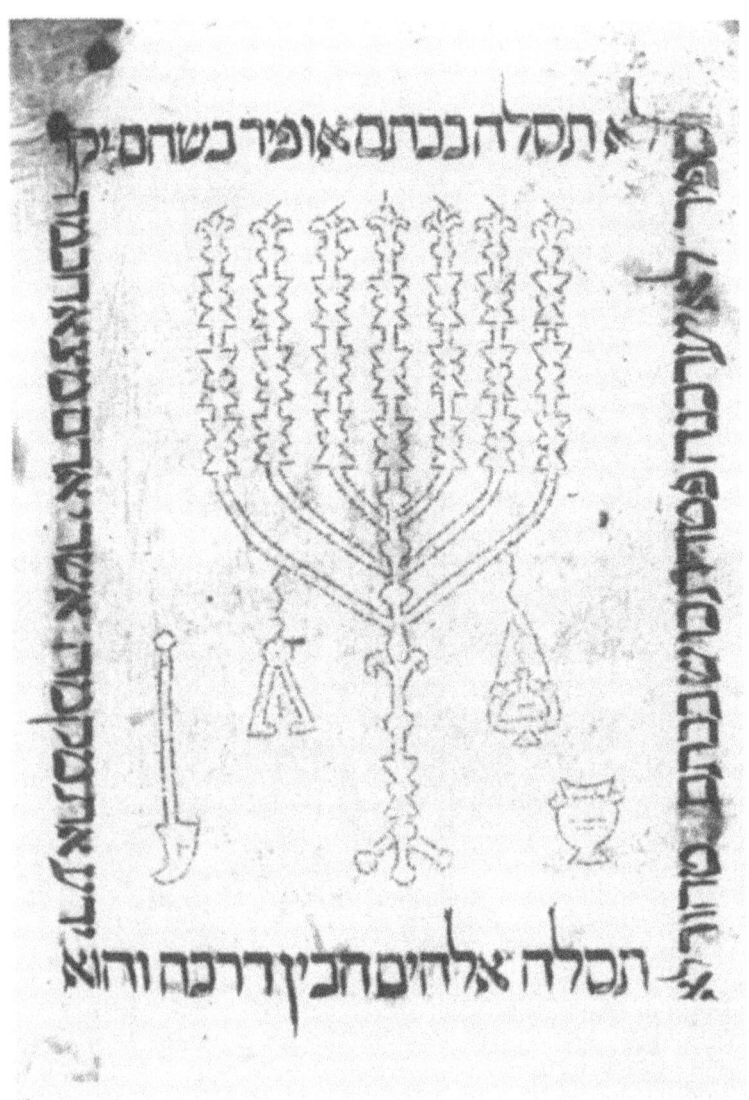

Figure 3

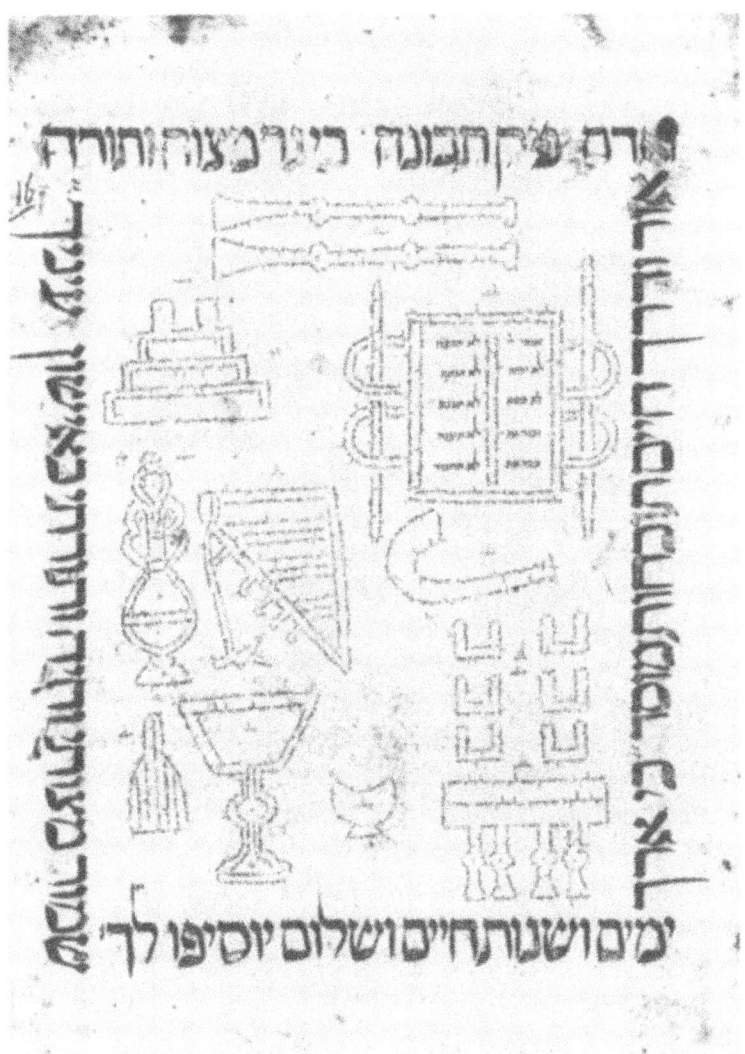

Figure 4

Figure 5

Figure 6

לֹא/לוֹ: AN ANALYSIS OF A KETHIB - QERE PHENOMENON

Abraham A. Lieberman
Yeshiva University

Masoretic lists[1] enumerate circa eighteen places in the Biblical Text where a Kethib-Qere of לֹא/לוֹ occurs. Its phonetical similarity and its orthographic disimilarity make this homophone[2] a unique phenomenon in the K-Q system. This K-Q has also been studied as the crux of the problem of dating the K-Q system. R. Gordis[3] used this K-Q at Job 13:15 in conjunction with the Mishna

---

1. Masorah Magna Leviticus 11:21, Sefer ᵓOklah Weᵓ-Oklah, Esteban edition: 139. Masorah Magna, Frensdorf: 247. While most lists enumerate only fifteen such cases and since the fifteen occurances are not identical the actual number is closer to twenty. See Ginzburg Intro. p. 428.

2. See Septuagint Genesis 26:32 where this homophone leads to a mistranslation. Already in 1692 Matthew Hiller commented that לֹא with *aleph* and לוֹ with *waw* are identical because *aleph* and *waw* are interchangeable. (D. Yellin in his commentary to Job [see 3:10] made many changes of *lamed aleph* into *lamed waw*, without sufficient proof.) Maimonides in his Commentary to the Mishna Sotah 5:5 quoting the early grammarians states that its phonetical similarity leads one to interpret the word with both meanings. See *Sepher Ha-Sherashim*, of Jonah Ibn Janach, Bacher Edition: 241, where this idea is also quoted in the name of Yehuda Ibn Hiyyug. See Ibn Ezra at Exodus 21:8 and at Psalms 100:3 in the name of R. Saadia Gaon for a similar opinion. B. Spinoza in his Theological-Political Tractate, chapter 9 (Heb. edition): 111, uses this K-Q as an example of a phonetical mix up. (My thanks to Philipe Cassuto, Université Jean Moulin, Lyon, for the Spinoza comment.)

3. R. Gordis, *The Biblical Text in the Making*, 1937:50. Later on in 1954 in an article printed in *Tarbiz* pp. 444-469, entitled "The Origin of the Masoretic Text in the Light of Rabbinic Literature and the Dead Sea Scrolls." Gordis qualified his position somewhat but on p. 462 used this K-Q as proof for its existence during the Yavneh Period as a K-Q, while maintaining that they were textual variants but not yet named K-Q.(!) His renewed position is undoubtedly due to Orlinsky's criticism. See n. 4.

Tractate Sotah 5:5 to state: "Long before the redaction of the Mishna this corpus (K-Q) of variants was complete." He concluded: "Here the Mishna is unable to decide between לא and לו apparently because both occur in the passage, the first as a Kethib and the second as a Qere. Orlinsky[4] in reviewing this book states: "Actually, however neither the Mishna nor the Gemara thereon makes any mention whatever of a K or Q; in other words, they knew them as textual variants, but not of a K-Q system."

If indeed R. Yeshua b. Hyrcanus (early 2nd century Tanna) in the above Mishna was referring to a K-Q, this would be the earliest mention in rabbinic literature of a K-Q.

One of the earliest lists of this particular K-Q is to be found in Tractate Sopherim 5:6,[5] which is of Palestinian provenance.[6] It enumerates three such instances in the Pentateuch: Leviticus 11:21, Leviticus 25:30, Exodus 21:8. The standard edition of the Talmud, the Vilna Edition, has parentheses around the last case as such: [יעדה] {יגיד} אשר לא to indicate that אשר לא יגיד (Leviticus 5:1) is a mistake and it should read אשר לא יעדה. The Tractate Sopherim, quoted by the Maḥzor Vitry[7] at this point, omits Exodus 21:8 while maintaining Leviticus 5:1. The critical edition of Tractate Sopherim[8] reads as follows after it lists the above

---

4. JAOS, 1940:42. W. F. Albright in his review of the Gordis book in JBL, LVII, 1938: 223-224 agreed with Orlinsky.

5. I should point out that in Tractate Sopherim, prior to the list, is the very famous rabbinical statement regarding the three scrolls deposited in the Temple Court, about which so much has been written. Dr. Orlinsky used this rabbinic passage in his now famous article on the origin of K-Q a new approach. Is it possible that the redactors of Tractate Sopherim connected this statement concerning the three scrolls with the list of לא/לו, because both have the common denominator of variant readings?

6. Zunz, *Die Gottesdienstlichen Vorträge Der Juden*, (Heb. edition): 47. As opposed to the Babylonian Tradition of the Masorah to Targum Onkelos, Berliner Edition, Leipzig, 1877:39 where Exodus 21:8, Leviticus 11:21 and Leviticus 25:30 are listed. For more information regarding the Palestinian origin of Tractate Sopherim, see Higger, Treatise Sopherim II, N.Y. 1930: 5-7.

7. Maḥzor Vitry, (a halakhic composition by R. Simcha Vitry, a pupil of Rashi who died before 1105), Horowitz Edition, Nerenberg 1923, Vol. 2: 696.

8. Treatise *Sopherim*, edited by Michel Higger, N.Y. 1930, reissued by Makor pub., Jerusalem, 1971: 172. The comment here is substantiated by eleven manuscripts. This is further strengthened by other rabbinical texts such as Yalkut Machiri (a 14th century midrashic collection), Isaiah, p. 72 not mentioned by Higger, footnote 26.

three cases: וריש אומרים אם לא יגיד. Leviticus 5:1 as a K-Q is not to my knowledge found in any extant reliable biblical manuscript, while undoubtedly at some time it was part of a Palestinian tradition. Kennicot, De Rossi, Ginzburg, BHK, make no mention of such a K-Q or variant. The more reliable Tiberian Manuscripts and the Textus Receptus read לרא, the plene spelling of the word.⁹

Leviticus 25:30 - בעיר אשר לא חומה - is found in all the lists. Yet upon closer analysis of the related rabbinical literature we see a different picture. The Siphra¹⁰ (a tannaitic halakhic Midrash to the Book of Leviticus) to this passage comments:

אשר לו חומה רבי אלעזר בר׳ יוסי אומר אשר לו חומה אע״פ
שאין לו עכשיו והיה לו לפנים מיכן

Rabbi Elazar, son of R. Yosi said: אשר לו חומה even though it has no wall now, as long as it had one, it is to be considered a walled city for all its laws. There is no mention of a K-Q here. Yet all commentators assume a K-Q at this spot, since indeed the statement here combines both meanings: (a) אשר לו - which has a wall to it. (b) what happens though if the wall is no longer there - אשר לא. He claims that the same laws still apply. In other words, even if now it doesn't have a wall (אשר לא) it is to be considered a walled city (אשר לו). No mention of a K-Q is made here. To solidify this point, the Palestinian Talmud¹¹ quoting Leviticus 25:30 (in a related law concerning a walled city) reads:

אשר לו חומה פרט לבית הבנוי בחומה רבי יהודה דרש אשר לו
חומה ר׳ שמעון דרש אשר לא חומה

The exact meaning of דרש is not clear. But what is clear is that no use was made of a K-Q. It could be this is part of the יש אם למקרא vs. יש אם למסורת argument. Yet had this been a K-Q you would expect to be told of it, not use the word דרש which usually means to expound, seek, etc.

The above mentioned Siphra, in all our extant manuscripts and prints, have the spelling *lamed waw*, yet in *all* editions in the margin we find a later correction that

---

9. Interesting to note that the Vilna edition of the Talmud at Shebuot 35A, quotes the defective spelling of לא and the plene spelling regarding this verse only two lines apart(!). See *Dikdukei Sopherim* (a work containing the variant readings to Talmudic literature) by R. N. Rabinowitz, Loco, footnotes 7-9, where most of this statement is lacking from the famous Munich Codex 95 of the Babylonian Talmud.

10. Siphra, the Jerusalem edition, 1959, with the commentaries of Rabad and R. Samson of Sens p. 117, the Koleditzky edition printed with the commentary of R. Hillel, Jerusalem 1961: 85. Also see Midrash Hagadol: 259.

11. Palestinian Talmud, Venice edition, Maaseroth 51A, Vilna edition 3: 4: 18a.

makes it read *lamed aleph,* based on the Masoretic list tradition. Interestingly enough, the medieval rabbinic commentator Rashi, at Arakin 32a where the Talmud quotes the same above Siphra, states:

לוא כתיב משמע לא ומשמע לו כלומר אין לו עכשיו והיה לו חומה קודם

In other words, Rashi's Biblical Text at Leviticus 25:30 read the plene spelling of *lamed waw aleph.* The Tosaphists on the spot comment after quoting Rashi:

ואינו כן בחומשין מדויקות כתב [לא באלף וקר׳ בוא״ו] {בוא״ו ולא קר׳ באלף}

Interestingly, the Tosaphists try to correct Rashi's text and the editors of the Vilna Talmud try to correct the Tosaphists' text.

Everything stated at Leviticus 25:30 can also be stated at Leviticus 11:18. In other words the Siphra[12] at this point repeats the words of the same Rabbi Eleazar b. Yosi:

אשר לו כרעים ר׳ אלעזר בן יוסי אמר אע״פ שאין לו עכשיו ועתיד לגדל לאחר זמן

Again no mention of a K-Q but a logical deduction of inference. This locust has no legs yet above its knee, (אשר לא), yet it will grow them soon, (אשר לו), but even at this infant stage it is to be considered edible.[13] In other words the K-Q in these two cases is an outgrowth of a midrashic inference. This can be seen even more clearly at the third instance of this particular K-Q at Exodus 21:8, אשר לא יעדה. The Mechilta of Rashbi[14] (a tannaitic halakhic Midrash to the Book of Exodus) states:

אשר לא יעדה מכלל לאו אתה שומע הן שאם רצה ליעד הרי מעיד

---

12. See note 10, Rabad Edition:52, Koleditzky Edition p. 78. Also see Midrash Haggadol (a 13th century Yemenite Rabbinic Midrash) p. 705 and the variants listed for line 9.

13. As above, all manuscripts here record a לו spelling. The same is true of Talmud Hullin 65A, where both the Talmudic and the Tosaphist texts are reverted by the editors to the לא spelling based on the masoretic tradition. See *Dikdukei Sopherim,* R. N. Rabinowitz, loco, footnote 300, where he testifies that all the talmudic manuscripts have a לו spelling.

14. Epstein-Melamed Edition, Jerusalem 1955: 166. The same can be seen from the comments found in The Mechilta of R. Yishmael, Horowitz Edition, Jerusalem, reissue, 1970:257, where all the *derashoth* (expositions) are based on a *lamed aleph* reading.

From the negative (לא אשר), you can state the positive (לו אשר), that if he wants to designate her, he can. No mention of a K-Q is made here, but it is clear that they read לו. It is very possible that in all these instances the rabbinic statement gave rise to this particular K-Q.

While the medieval rabbinic attitude accepted all these instances as a K-Q, the great medieval commentator R. Abraham Ibn Ezra at Exodus 21:8 states emphatically in his classical style:[15]

ודע כי לו קר׳ וכתוב הוא בפנים באלף ובחוץ בוא״ו ...
והנכון בעיני כי זה השני היא האמת לבדו וככה כולם

This K-Q becomes even more interesting at Job 6:21:

כי עתה הייתם לו תראו. The Leningrad B19a reads לא as a K, with לו as a Q. The Yemenite versions[16] have לא with no mention of a Q. The popular editions such as Koren[17] have לו with no mention of a Q. To make matters more unclear, some Masoretic lists[18] enumerate this K-Q as a point of contention between the Easterners who read לא, with the Westerners reading לו. To really cloud the issue, Mishael b. Uzziel[19] tells us here, that this was one of the differences between Ben Asher who read לא, and Ben Naphtali who read לו. Norzi dismisses this from a K-Q system since it is not part of the fifteen enumerated by the Massora Magna at Leviticus 11:21.[20]

---

15. Ibn Ezra reiterates his point again at Leviticus 11:18.

16. See also *The Commentary of R. Saadia Gaon to Job*, Jerusalem 1973, edited by Rabbi Joseph Kapiach with a Yemenite Text of Job:59, footnote 21, also Job 41:4 in the above sources. (No luck from the Job Qumran Targum as it omits all our passages.)

17. Credit should be given to the new edition of "The *Daat Mikra* series" and the valuable comments of R. Mordecai Breuer in his preparation of each volume and its Masoretic variants. See "*Daat Mikra*" *Job*, Jerusalem, 1981:35, notes on Job 6:21 and p. 52 footnote 34.

18. See Norzi, Loco.

19. Lazar Lipschütz "*Kitab Al-Khilaf*, The Book of The Ḥillufim, Mishael Ben Uzziel's Treatise on the Differences Between Ben Asher and Ben Naphtali," *Textus*, Vol. IV, 1964: 16 footnote 2, and in the actual text published by the HUBP, Jerusalem, p. 50.

20. Norzi consistently sticks to the fifteen cases of the Massorah Magna. See Norzi at Joshua 5:14, 1 Chron 5:1, 11:20.

The Genizah fragments[21] which I have examined in researching this paper, in general fall into place in comparison with the variants listed by Ginzburg. In all the instances, some manuscripts have לא as a K-Q, some have לו as a K-Q, some have לא as a K and לו as a Q and vice versa. One interesting Genizah fragment (T-S A.11.14) at Job 6:21 has לא as a K with no Q, while (T-S 18A1) had לו with no K-Q on the margin. Yet someone (at a closer look) wrote a *waw* over the *aleph*. In other words it becomes quite evident that until very late at Job 6:21 we have a text in a state of flux.

To return to Job 13:15, the Talmud at Sotah 31a, where the question is asked: וליחזי האי לא אי בלמד אלף etc., is a stammaitic statement, showing its Savoraic provenance, therefore quite late and one is unable to date it. Yet with its response of משמע הכי ומשמע הכי the talmudic masters tell us that the phonetical similarity of לו/לא would lead one to always interpret this homophone with both possibilities. This undoubtedly gave rise to some of the K-Q of this sort.

Now with the discovery of D.S.S. we see the plene spelling of לוא in about 80% of the instances. For example, at Isaiah 49:5 (not listed in the Masorah Magna) where again we have a K-Q of לא-לו, the D.S.S. read לו, yet at Isaiah 9:2, at 63:9, the D.S.S. read לוא, yet the Yemenite manuscripts read לא at Isaiah 63:9.

The phonetical similarity between לו/לא , quite undistinguishable to a listener (unless he reads it along with the reader from a written text or from contextual surmizing), undoubtedly led to some mix up, regarding the evolvement of this K-Q. As much as it seems, some arose out of a rabbinical/ midrashic system. I have not listed the rabbinical medieval commentators[22] to all the passages which quite clearly at times read either לא or לו. For example, R. Joseph Kimchi regarding Psalms 139:15 states:

ולו אחד בהם אמר מנחם ואין לו, ולא ידעתי אם הוא אצלו באלף או בוא״ו

---

21. For Leviticus 25:30 see OR 1080 A. 1315, T-S Misc 24:86, T-S A3, 13, T-S A26, 76, 115, 150, 155, 213. Proverbs 26:2 see T-S A12, 6, 7. Leviticus 5:1 see T-S A34.12, T-S A2:22, T-S Misc 2.26. Special thanks to Dr. E. J. Revell and his *Biblical Texts With Palestinian Pointing and Their Accents*, Masoretic Studies 4: 239-241 for 3 additional Genizah fragments dealing with this particular K-Q. Also see T-S A2:18 for Exodus 21:8, Leviticus 11:21 see T-S A3.20, 21.

22. For example see R. Meyuhas b. Elijah on Job 41:4. Also Nahmanides, Ha-Meiri at Proverbs 19:7, 26:2 and more. The comments of R. Joseph Kimchi are found in *Sepher Ha-Galui*, H. J. Matthew, Berlin 1887: 113.

At this point Psalms Q. Cave 11 reads לו and both readings, as in all instances, have manuscript variants backing them up. It is quite clear that K-Q of לו/לא cannot be used as evidence that the Tannaim already knew of this K-Q. It is clear though, that rabbinical literature, where these texts were used and studied, can help trace the steps of the development of K-Q.

LIST OF לו/לא KETHIV-QERE

1. Exod 21:8 Found in all lists.
   LXX reading the Q with Sam. and Syr. reading the K. See Norzi's comments here.
2. Lev 11:21 Found in all lists.
   LXX, Sam. and Syr. read Q.
3. Lev 25:30 Found in all lists.
   LXX. Sam. and Syr. read Q. See Norzi's comments here.
4. 1 Sam 2:3   LXX reads Q.
5. 2 Sam 16:18   LXX reads Q.
6. 2 Sam 18:12   LXX reads Q.
7. 2 Sam 19:7   LXX reads Q.
8. 2 Kgs 8:10   LXX reads Q.
9. Isa 9:2   LXX reads Q.
10. Isa 49:5 Not in the Mm list. See ᵓOklah we-ᵓOklah, Esteban edition:139.
11. Isa 63:9   LXX read לא צר, see Norzi's comments.
12. Job 6:21 Leningrad B19A, see Norzi's comments, and my comments above.
13. Job 13:15 All Lists. See above.
10. Job 41:4 See Norzi's comments.
   LXX reads Q.
15. Ps 110:3   LXX reads Q, but see comments in the *Anchor Bible*.
16. Ps 139:16   LXX reads Q. See Midrash Haggadol, Num 10:35. Line 5 and variants.
17. Prov 19:7   LXX reads Q.
18. Prov 26:2   LXX reads Q.
19. Ezra 4:2   LXX reads Q.
20. 1 Chr 11:20 See 2 Sam 23:18, where no K-Q appears.
   Missing in Mm, see Ginsburg, Intro. p. 428.

Masoretic lists also enumerate two instances of *lamed waw* to be read as *lamed aleph*:
    1 Sam 2:16 and 1 Sam 20:2.
See also
    (1) Jos 5:14 and the comments of Norzi there (and also the *Anchor Bible* and its commentary.
    (2) 1 Chron 5:1 and Genesis Rabba, Theodor Albeck edition, vol. 2: 989.
    (3) Num 23:23. See Norzi's comments.

THE LATEST SPANISH CONTRIBUTION TO MASORETIC RESEARCH

Mª Teresa Ortega-Monasterio
Instituto de Filología, CSIC - Madrid

At the kind request of Prof. Orlinsky, I am going to make a report on the Spanish contribution to the critical editions of the Bible, during the last two decades.

One of the greatest works of Spanish humanism in the 16th century was the edition of the Complutensian Polyglot, committed by Cardenal Cisneros to Alcalá University. In that century, and at the request of Philip II, another polyglot, the so called Biblia Regia, was edited by Arias Montano in Antwerp.

Conscious of this brilliant Spanish tradition in the field of biblical philology, a group of humanists undertook, about forty years ago, an ambitious project sponsored by the C.S.I.C.: the edition of a new Polyglot Bible, according to modern criticism. This task required a complex planning depending on the *status quo* of the biblical criticism of the different languages and led to a publication in independent volumes, because of the complexity of the texts to be edited. The work was assumed by the former Instituto Arias Montano, now Department of Biblical Philology and Ancient Near East of the Institute of Philology of the C.S.I.C. This project yielded fruits of major scientific interest, both in the studies of the old languages included in the Polyglot (I shall speak later about this) and in the very edition of their corresponding biblical texts. In order to publish all these works, the Department took charge of the series "Textos y Estudios Cardenal Cisneros" of the C.S.I.C. in which almost fifty volumes have been published.

First of all, I am going to give a brief exposition of all the groups working in this Department, including the achievements and projects of each one of them. Afterwards, I will focus my attention on the Hebrew Bible team, which is the main subject of this paper. I think it is interesting to include here this general review of the rest of the teams, because we are all closely connected and our projects are interrelated.

The Department of Biblical Philology and Ancient Near East is basically composed of three research teams: Hebrew Bible, Greek Bible and Aramaic Bible.

Recently, a new scholarly specialist in Ancient Near Eastern studies has been incorporated. Occasionally, some young doctors join the different teams of the Department, being a great help for the development of our work. The whole Department has been integrated since 1974 in different projects, sponsored by the CAICYT. This has made possible the publication of most of our works. The project we are working on now is entitled "Edition of Biblical and Parabiblical Texts" (Biblia Políglota Matritense), and it is headed by Prof. Natalio Fernández Marcos. Other teams are also taking part in this project, such as those of the Latin, Coptic and Armenian Bible. Our main purpose is to publish unedited sources of biblical and parabiblical literature. Within the next three years, the concrete goal of the different teams is the publication of eleven volumes concerning the different fields of research.

Although the different teams have a common methodology basic to the edition of texts in ancient languages, the editorial procedures differ, depending on the peculiar problems of each language. The development and the practice of textual criticism, as we know, is not the same in the Greek and Latin biblical texts as it is in the Semitic languages. That is why every team must be aware of the problems of editing, according to the language of the texts to be edited.

As a pioneering work, and concerning the edition of Aramaic-targumic texts, we have the Editio Princeps of the manuscript Neophyti 1, in six volumes, carried out by Prof. Díez Macho in collaboration with some scholars of his team. This work, in total about a thousand pages of unpublished Aramaic text with critical apparatus, was published by the C.S.I.C. This edition has given rise to great interest in our scientific world due to the fact that it was an unknown text recovered by the late Prof. Díez Macho, who was one of the first world authorities in these studies.

The aim of the Aramaic Texts project is to offer all the researchers new manuscripts recently discovered in different libraries all around the world, which represent the authentic tradition of this Aramaic-targumic literature. This team is going to publish the Targum Onkelos of Leviticus-Numbers, based on MS 448 of the Vatican Library, which reflects the most authentic phonetics of the Babylonian Aramaic; a distinction between first and second hand is made and the parallelism between this text and Sabioneta Onkelos is established. They have also edited the texts of the Targum Jonathan of Samuel and Isaiah, based on the best Babylonian Aramaic manuscripts not yet published, making a comparative study of the readings on which the texts agree. With the same methodology, the critical editions of the Targum of Job, Joshua-Judges, Kings, Jeremiah and Songs will also be prepared.

The interest of these texts lies in the fact that they mainly belong to a group of writings which are mostly dated in the first years of the Christian Era and they are very important for the study of our Judeo-Christian culture.

As these documents are mostly unpublished, they provide new data for the comparative study of the different stages of the Aramaic language. The Aramaic school of targumic studies is internationally well-known due to its long and deep devotion and its large number of publications. Now, we shall consider the different parts of the project:

First: the already mentioned study of MS 448 of the Vatican Library.

Second: the Targum Jonathan of Joshua, Judges, Samuel and Kings based on MS 229 of the Jewish Theological Seminary of New York, including the various readings of the different manuscripts of Babylonian punctuation from the Cairo Genizah, kept in Oxford and Cambridge. We would like to thank Prof. Yeivin for giving permission to consult his filmotheque. Dr. Martínez Borobio is responsible for this work.

Prof. Ribera Florit, of the University of Barcelona, has been charged to prepare unpublished MS materials, representing to the Isaiah Targum in Babylonian Aramaic. Besides this, Prof. Vallina will study the best targumic MSS of Alfonso de Zamora, kept in the University Library in Salamanca, and also the MS Heb 110 of the National Library in Paris.

Concerning the Greek text, the most important antecedents are *Theodoreti Cyrensis Quaestiones in Octateuchum* (Madrid 1979) and *Quaestiones in Reges et Paralipomena* (Madrid 1984) by some members of the corresponding team. These works constitute the first step in undertaking the edition of the Antiochian text of the Greek Bible in the books where it is clearly determined, namely the books of Samuel and Kings. The interest of the Antiochian text is obvious; it keeps an old tradition of the Greek Bible, closely related to the different fragments of the book of Samuel found in Qumran cave 4. It has relevant consequences for the history of the text of Samuel and Kings. Their differences with the traditional Hebrew text have incidence mostly on questions about chronology and traditions during the monarchic period in Israel.

This is the first critical edition of this text (although Lagarde published it in 1883 but in a form which was deficient and without a critical apparatus). It incorporates the new achievements of the edition of the *Quaestiones in Reges et Paralipomena of Theodoretus*, which is the best control of this biblical text. It also incorporates the new edition of the Palimpsestus Vindobonensis, published by Fischer and Ulrich in the IOSCS 16th Bulletin (1983); it constitutes the main uninterrupted text of the Vetus Latina for the books of Samuel-Kings. They will also incorporate the results of a new study of the marginal notes in the Codex Legionensis (960), as the editor of such notes, C. Vercellone (1864) used a flawed copy of this codex, kept in the Vatican Library. Finally, another important contribution is the incorporation of the Armenian readings of the Bible into the apparatus. This

Armenian work has been carried out by Prof. P. Cowe, of the City College, Columbia University. Up to now, the current edition of the Armenian Bible was Zohrab's edition (1808), and since then many new MSS have changed the image of this edition. The oldest stage of the Armenian version, as it works with Vetus Latina, is very close to the Antiochian Text of the Septuagint.

Concerning the Greek project, Dr. Natalio Fernández Marcos and Dr. José Ramón Busto Saiz have undertaken the collation and the study of the Greek Bible MSS bearing an Antiochian text, the quotations of the Antiochian fathers and Vetus Latina, which are to be incorporated into the apparatus, and also the references to the Hebrew text and Qumran text. They have also been given the responsibility of establishing the definite text and of writing the general introduction to the work. Dra. Mª Victoria Spottorno has been given the task of the identification and study of Flavius Josephus' quotations in connection with the Antiochian text. Prof. P. Cowe bases the Armenian version on the study of about fifteen MSS; he is already preparing the books of Samuel. Finally, Dr. J. Trebolle studies the Vetus Latina in the books of Samuel-Kings, in relationship with the Septuagint and Hebrew texts. This combined study of higher and lower criticism is producing interesting results.

Although the Latin team has been recently created, it already has a brilliant tradition through the works of the late Prof. Ayuso Marazuela, an old member of this project; all these works have been published between 1953 and 1967. This team has collected the MSS and evaluated all the material in order to edit the marginal notes of Vetus Latina in the Spanish Bibles. The interest of this project is based on the fact that our libraries and Public Record Offices are very rich in Vulgates with marginal notes of Vetus Latina: some of them have already been published by Prof. Ayuso Marazuela; more recently, in 1980, Prof. Ziegler published the notes to Job, but most of them are still unpublished.

Dr. Aranda, editor of the Coptic texts, has been working with one of the best specialists in Coptic language, Prof. Orlandi, of the University of Milan. He has already published two volumes, the Gospels of Matthew and Mark, based on the codex Pierpont Morgan 569.

Now, I shall enter into the main purpose of this paper, the description of the work of the Hebrew Bible team. It consists now of four members; at first the team was headed by Prof. Pérez Castro, but since 1979 Dra. Fernández Tejero has taken over this role. From the beginning its main purpose was to publish the *Editio Princeps* of the Cairo Codex of the Prophets. This edition tries to reproduce the codex as exactly as possible, with no modification, either in its text, or in its masorah. Due to the economic problems that this edition presented, we had to make an offset edition. As it does not pretend to be a facsimile edition, the text has not been typed in three columns; nevertheless, we maintained the open and closed sections and every graphic sign, even the *rafeh* and the position of the *meteg*.

In the first critical apparatus we include the dubious, anomalous and clearly erroneous readings. This way, the scholar is sure of facing the original text of the codex, if we can speak of certainty in a critical edition.

In the second critical apparatus we have developed the masorah magna and parva, identifying the corresponding *sîmanîm*, and following BH3 in the books missing in the Cairo codex. So, we provide for the scholars a very correct textual and masoretical tradition, based on a classic codex in the history of the biblical text. The purpose of editing both masoras together is to closely connect them, and make their comparative study easy. The relationship between text and apparatus is shown by the corresponding *circelli*.

A third critical apparatus includes the explanatory notes to the second one. Needless to say, the vocalization, both in the text and in the apparatuses, has been written by hand.

Following this scheme, from 1979 to 1988 we have published the seven projected volumes of our edition.

As for the difficulties presented by the work, they have been clearly explained in the paper presented by Dra. Fernández Tejero at the fifth congress of the IOMS (Salamanca 1983), "Report on Cairo Codex Edition".[1] Now, I just would like to point out that the initial presuppositions of the work had to be changed in an important way: although for the first two published volumes (Minor Prophets and Joshua-Judges), Dra. Fernández Tejero and I could consult, in May 1978, the original MS kept in the Abbasiyya Synagogue in Cairo, when we tried to go to Cairo again in 1981, the authorities of the Karaite community denied us permission to work with the codex without giving any reason. According to rumour that has been going round for some time, perhaps it has been sold to another community to use it exclusively and publish it. But up to now, we have not had any news about the whole question.

Consequently, for the other volumes we had to use the microfilms and the photographs taken by Prof. Beit Arié, and kept in the Hebrew University Library in Jerusalem. Although this edition is already concluded, I ask you the same questions Dra. Fernández Tejero asked in Salamanca: Could anybody give us news about the Cairo Codex? Where is it? Has it been sold? If so, to whom? It would be exciting to touch it again, to have it again before us, even if only for a moment, after such a long

---

1. *Estudios Masoréticos*, ed. por E. Fernández Tejero, *Textos y Estudios* 33, Madrid 1983: 79-86.

time. Having worked with it every day, for a whole month, and under such conditions, we really became fond of it.

But coming back to our projects, we are planning to publish in two years a volume including the masoretical indices of the whole work. For this task, we rely upon our team of four women. This is the moment to thank Prof. Orlinsky, our dear President, and all the members of our organization, for the encouragement and help they have always offered us.

But we have not dedicated ourselves exclusively to the edition of the Cairo Codex. One of our main fields of research has been, and still is, the study of the Spanish codices, because of their traditionally accepted importance. We can already find in the 10th century, references to the "old and accurate Spanish Bibles" (*Tešubot Talmide Menaḥem ben Saruq* to the *Dibre Dunaš ben Labraṭ*). Zimmels mentioned the high opinion the Askenazim had of the Sephardic codices (*Askenazim and Sephardim*, London 1958), and he also quoted the testimony of Menaḥem ha Meʾirí, who speaks about the famous R. Samuel ben Jacob who travelled from Germany to Toledo to buy a Pentateuch copied from a scroll which was written by R. Meʾir ha-Leví, according to all the rules required by a *Sefer Torah*.

Menaḥem de Lonzano also had a high opinion of them, as well as Y. S. de Norzi, who mentioned the existence of correct codices brought from Jerusalem to Spain. He even used a manuscript dated in Toledo in 1277 to prepare his edition of the Bible. It was precisely the importance given by Norzi to the Sephardic codices that led N. H. Snaith to base his edition of the Bible on Sephardic MSS in which he tried to find the Ben Asher text.

For all these reasons, and also to continue with the Alcalá tradition, where Sephardic codices were used in the Hebrew column of the Complutensian Polyglot, basically the MSS M1 and M2 of the Madrid University Library, we have included the study of these Spanish codices among our fields of research. These studies have given rise to a number of books plus a great number of articles.

The general conclusion of these works is that, if we could not really speak about the existence of a Scriptorium Toletanum, we could demonstrate that the fame of the Spanish codices was undoubtedly well-grounded, since these codices agree closely with the Tiberian tradition of Ben Asher, although this agreement is smaller than that which they present among themselves.

In contrast to the variant, anomalous and irregular readings of the Askenazic codices, the Sephardic textual biblical tradition offers a high degree of uniformity, and a close agreement with the accurate Tiberian tradition.

Following this method of research, other similar works are now being prepared, such as the translation and critical notation of *Minḥat Šay* in the book of Isaiah and the whole translation of the *ʾOr Tôrah*.

I hope I have clearly explained the project we are engaged in, the task of each team and the works we are publishing.

And, as Lonzano literally wrote, at the end of his *'Or Tôrah*,

ולכן בכל דבר שיסתפק אדם בכל המקרא, אם ישאל את פי בע״ה,
אברר ספקו ובפרט, אם אהיה בביתי.

I deeply thank you all, not only for the warm acceptance that our works have always received, but also for the attention you have given me today. Thank you very much.

CONJUNCTIVE DAGESH: A PRELIMINARY STUDY

E. J. Revell
University of Toronto

The term "Conjunctive Dagesh" is used here to cover both the phenomena traditionally referred to as *deḥîq*, and those referred to as *ʾatê meraḥîq*.[1] The descriptions of these phenomena in the standard grammars, such as those of Gesenius-Kautzsch, Bergsträsser, or Joüon, are based on that of S. Baer. Baer sees the phenomenon as following set rules, with very few exceptions. Even in the limited range of examples which he gives, however, there are many variants from the Leningrad Codex B19a (L). The description given by I. Yeivin is less inclined to see the phenomenon as following fixed rules, and admits a considerable number of exceptions in some situations. This description is less complex than is Baer's, having merged some of the categories set up by Baer. However its use of the masoretic definition of vocal *shewa*, and its treatment of the use of *maqqef* separately from the use of a conjunctive accent seems to complicate the description unnecessarily.[2]

Conjunctive *dagesh* typically occurs where a word ending in an unstressed open syllable with the vowel *qameṣ* or *segol* (terminal, or followed by *he*), and marked with a conjunctive accent or *maqqef*, is followed by a word stressed on its first full vowel

---

1. I had originally intended to use the term *deḥîq* to cover both (following the uggestion of Dotan "The Problem of *Deḥîq* and *Até Méraḥîq*" *Fourth World Congress of ewish Studies, Papers*, Vol. II [Jerusalem, 1969]: 101-105 [Hebrew], 186 [English ummary] about its original meaning), but since most descriptions use both terms in he traditional way, this seems unwise.

2. For Baer's description see "De primarum vocabulorum literarum agessatione" (in his *Liber Proverbiorum*, Lipsiae, 1880: vii-xiii). For that of Yeivin, see is *Introduction to the Tiberian Masorah*, Missoula, 1980, #404-405. Yeivin's description based on A.

(i.e. C¹V-- or C∂C¹V--, etc.). A pair of words with these characteristics is referred to here as a "standard pair". Where such a pair occurs, *dagesh* may be marked in the first letter of the second word. This "conjunctive *dagesh*" is never used in initial *alef, he, ḥet, ʿayin,* or *waw*, so cases in which the second word begins with one of these letters are not considered as examples of a "standard pair". In L, conjunctive *dagesh* is not used after a word ending in *alef* in the Hebrew text (as far as I know -- including אַל־תֵּרֶא יַיִן in Prov 23:31, mentioned in Yeivin's #404), but is used several times in the Aramaic parts of Daniel and Ezra (which are not extant in A), as כְּלָּא מְטָא (Dan 4:25), אָמְרְנָא לְהֹם (Ezra 5:4, 9). These Aramaic examples are not considered here. The special case of מָה is also ignored. Apart from these, I have noted only 28 cases (less than 1/3 of 1%) in which conjunctive *dagesh* is used in a situation different from that of the standard pair defined above.[3]

It appears from a survey of the standard pairs collected that, when other conditions are the same, it makes no difference to the use of conjunctive *dagesh* whether the two words are joined by a conjunctive accent or by *maqqef*. Consequently the two situations are not distinguished. It also appears that *shewa* is most usefully classified according to whether it does or does not reflect an earlier vowel. When the material is treated in this way, the basic pattern of occurrence of conjunctive *dagesh* can be described very simply. Conjunctive *dagesh* typically occurs in three categories of standard pairs:

    1.   Where the first word ends in *segol*. 231 of 242 cases (95%), as Gen 2:18 אֶעֱשֶׂה־לּוֹ.

    2.   Where the first word ends in *qames*, if that *qames* is typically not stressed in the contextual form of that word. 304 of 330 cases 92%), as Gen 12:18 הִגַּדְתָּ־לִּי.

    3.   Where the first word ends in *qames* preceded by a *shewa* which is marked as vocal, or reflects an earlier vowel. 153 of 178 cases (86%) as Gen 18:21 אֵרֲדָה־נָּא.

In category 3, the final *qames* is typically stressed in the contextual form. In a fourth category, the other cases in which the first word of a standard pair ends in *qames* which is typically stressed in the contextual form, conjunctive *dagesh* typically does not occur. 170 of 184 cases (92%), as Gen 4:6 חָרָה לָךְ.

---

3. Conjunctive *dagesh* occurs in a few cases in which the first word of the pair has final stress (Yeivin, op. cit. #405, end) and (more commonly) where the second word is not stressed on its first syllable (ibid. #407.i, see also #4 below). The presence or absence of *ga ya* is of no significance in L in the latter cases (see ibid. #406).

The list of examples of conjunctive *dagesh* from which these figures are taken was generated by computer search of the FCAT text of the Bible in transliteration. The problems of using this text for a search of this sort were not fully solved; a hand search revealed about 10% more examples. This hand search has been carried out over Genesis, and the text extant in A. Consequently the list of examples used in this preliminary study is not complete, but should be nearly so. The material was studied in L, and the usage of L in the examples collected was compared with A and C.[4] These codices rarely differ from L save in a few cases where they use conjunctive *dagesh* according to the standard pattern, but L fails to use it. Some of these cases are noted below. In one case, however, all three sources differ. In שֶׁם וּבָאת (2 Kgs 9:2), A has *gaʿya* and *maqqef* on the verb, and shows conjunctive *dagesh*. L has *tifḥa* and does not show *dagesh*. Both, then, are consistent with the standard pattern. C also shows *tifḥa* on the verb, and shows *dagesh* in the first letter of the following word. This *dagesh* is anomalous (since the first word of the pair has a disjunctive) looks like the result of conflation. There are a few other cases in which it seems possible that the use of conjunctive *dagesh* developed in a form of the tradition slightly different from that shown in these codices. Among the most persuasive are:

Jud 6:39   אָנַסֶּה נָּא־רַק־הַפַּעַם
Ps 118:25 הוֹשִׁיעָה נָּא ... הַצְלִיחָה נָּא

The figures for the standard categories given above show that the use of conjunctive *dagesh* is much more regular than is generally supposed. This impression is strengthened by a consideration of the exceptions. Many of these fall into groups which can be defined morphologically, and undoubtedly reflect inaccuracy in the description rather than irregularity in the phenomenon. Thus the fourteen exceptions in category 4 are all 2m.s perfect forms with *waw* consecutive, as Deut 27:7

---

4. Facsimiles of these sources are published as follows: L as *Pentateuch, Prophets, and Hagiographa: Codex Leningrad B19a* with an introduction by D. S. Loewinger, Jerusalem, 1970; A as *The Aleppo Codex* ed. by M. H. Goshen Gottstein, Jerusalem, 1976; C as *The Cairo Codex of the Prophets* ed. by D. S. Loewinger, Jerusalem, 1971. P, *Prophetarum posteriorum codex babylonicus Petropolitanus* ed. H. Strack, St. Petersburg, 1881, was also compared, as was *The Old Testament ... with the Various Readings from the MSS* (ed. by C. D. Ginsburg, London, 1926). Some of the variations from L shown by P may be systematic, but neither these, nor those recorded by Ginsburg (which do not appear to be systematic) are significant for the present purpose.

וְזָבַחְתָּ שְׁלָמִים וְאָכַלְתָּ שָּׁם.[5] That is, in the matter of conjunctive *dagesh*, the perfect with *waw* consecutive acts like a "simple" perfect, a member of category 2.

The question of whether a word ending in *qames* typically has final or penultimate stress in contextual position is not always clear. Apart from 2m.s forms of perfect with *waw* consecutive, however, it is always possible to give a plausible answer consistent with the pattern shown in the standard categories. As far as I know, the only case where such an answer differs from the commonly accepted view of the form is that of מָרָה־לָּהּ (2 Kgs 4:27). The first word of the pair is usually categorized as a perfect verb form.[6] In this case stress would be typically penultimate and *dagesh* is expected. The form could equally well be an adjective. In this case typical stress would be final, and the lack of conjunctive *dagesh* in the following לָּהּ would conform to the expected pattern. Typical final stress is also assumed for שִׂמְחָה (Amos 1:11. The final *he* represents a pronoun), and (with less certainty) אֹרְיָה (Ps 120:5). Unusual forms for which typical penultimate stress is assumed are הָרָה (Gen 30:1, etc.);[7] רָבָה (2 Sam 24:6, the final *he* is "directional"); and וְהִנִּיחָה (Zech 5:11, with stress position corresponding to that of the *hif'il*). Typical penultimate stress for the noun forms like יְשׁוּעָתָה (Ps 3:3), עֶזְרָתָה (Ps 44:27), עַרְלָתָה (Ps 92:16), בַּצָּרָתָה (Ps 120:1) is amply demonstrated in nouns of this form elsewhere (Exod 15:16, Ezek 28:15, Jonah 2:10, etc.). It can reasonably be stated, then, that in category 4, where the first word of a standard pair ends in *qames* which is typically stressed in context and is not preceded by *shewa* reflecting an earlier vowel, the failure to use conjunctive *dagesh* is absolutely regular.

Where the first word of a standard pair ends in *qames* which is typically not stressed in context, the largest group of exceptions to the common pattern (I have 13 examples) occurs where the second word of the pair has a prefixed preposition (-בְּ or

---

5. Exod 25:12, Lev 25:35, Deut 14:26, 16:2, 17:14, 26:1, 27:7, 28:36, 64, 2 Sam 9:10, 1 Kgs 22:13, Ezek 28:12, 35:3, 2 Chron 18:12. These are all from strong roots. *Waw* consecutive perfect forms from final weak roots do not usually develop final stress.

6. So, e.g., the Lexicon of Brown, Driver and Briggs, also that of Koehler, Baumgartner, et. al., also A. Even-Shoshan, *A New Concordance of the Bible* (Jerusalem, 1982).

7. This would be irregular of the root is יהב, but the imperative of נגשׁ shows similar forms with penultimate stress beside the expected patterns. Identical forms of imperative (of different origin) occur in אָרָה (Num 22:6), and קָבָה (Num 22:11).

-לְ -- a well-known phenomenon, although not so consistent as is sometimes suggested).

In the second largest group of exceptions in category 2, the first word is a feminine plural imperfect form from a final weak root with *segol* as its penultimate stressed vowel. I have noted six examples, as וַתִּהְיֶינָה לִּי (Ezek 23:4).[8] C agrees with L in not showing conjunctive *dagesh* here, as does A in all six cases. It is difficult to see how these exceptions could have a phonological basis. Conjunctive *dagesh* does occur after a word ending in stressed *segol* followed by *qames* where the two vowels are separated by *nun* marked with *dagesh*, as with the suffixes in 1 Sam 18:21, 21:10, etc., and even in Mic 7:10 תִּרְאֶינָּה בָּהּ. It also occurs where vowels are separated by a single consonant other than *nun* as in Gen 14:10, 38:29, Jos 8:28, etc. It is remarkable, however, that f.pl imperfect verbs commonly form exceptions to other standard phonological patterns. Neither the change of original *a to *qames* in pause, nor the change of original *i to *patah* in a closed stressed syllable, occurs regularly in these forms.[9] What connection, if any, this has with the development of conjunctive *dagesh* is a matter for speculation.

In a number of other other exceptions to the standard pattern in category 2, conjunctive *dagesh* does not occur in L where A and C do show it. Most of these reflect the tendency in L, noted by Prof. Dotan, to omit *dagesh* in initial שׁ, מ, etc., where the second letter of the word has *dagesh*.[10] Of the other cases of omission of expected *dagesh*, in L at least, וּבְאָזְנֶיךָ שְׁמָע (Ezek 3:10) appears to be an error. L does show *dagesh* in the same pair in Ezek 40:4, 44:5; A and C show it in all three cases. In fact, there are only two cases in L in category 2 which do not appear clearly

---

8. Also forms from קרא in Ruth 1:20, 20, 21, 4:17, 17. Conjunctive *dagesh* occurs regularly in f.pl imperfect forms where the penultimate syllable is closed, as תֶּלְבַּ֫כְןָ מָ֫יִם (Ezek 7:17), and also where that syllable is open with *holem* in וַתָּבֹ֫אנָה לָּ֑ךְ in L, (Isa 47:9) A, C.

9. *Patah* reflects original *a in the stressed syllable of an f.pl imperfect form in pause in Isa 5:15, 32:3, 60:14, Jer 49:2, Mic 7:16, and even before *ayin* in תִּשְׁבַּ֫עְנָה (Prov. 27:20, 20, 30:15). As far as I know, *qames* occurs only in תִּישַׁ֫מְנָה (Ezek 6:6). *Sere* occurs regularly in the stressed syllable of f.pl imperfect forms from *pi*el or *hif*il stems, and in the *qal* form תָּגֵ֫לְנָה (Ps 48:12, 51:10, 97:8). The expected *patah* occurs in other *qal* forms, as תֶּלְבַּ֫כְןָ, and in *nif*al forms.

10. See A. Dotan, "Deviation in Gemination in the Tiberian Vocalization", *Estudios Masoreticos*, ed. E. Fernández-Tejero (Textos y Estudios vol. 33, 1983):67.

to result from conditioning (phonological or otherwise) or error, and even these may be explicable.

Neither the few exceptions in category 1, nor the many in category 3, show such clear evidence of conditioning, but it seems probable that some, at least, were conditioned. In category 1, where a standard pair is formed of אֵלֶּה followed by a preposition with a pronominal suffix, as מָה־אֵלֶּה לָּךְ (2 Sam 16:2, and similarly Gen 33:5, 38:25, Ezek 24:19, 39:18), conjunctive *dagesh* is used. Where the second word is a noun or adverb, as וְאֵלֶּה שְׁמוֹת בְּנֵי־לֵוִי (Exod 6:16, and similarly Gen 46:8, Deut 5:3, Isa 47:9), conjunctive *dagesh* is not used. It seems likely that in this latter group the prosodic patterns defining the structures originally prevented the development of conjunctive *dagesh*. That is to say, they were different from those reflected by the received accentuation. It is noteworthy that, in the 17 other cases where אֵלֶּה שְׁמוֹת is followed by a noun or noun phrase, אֵלֶּה has a disjunctive accent, and so cannot form a standard pair. In category 3, nouns in which the penultimate syllable was originally closed by a guttural which is followed by a *ḥatef shewa* in L act in the same way as do nouns in which a simple *shewa* in the same position is considered silent, as נַחֲלָה־לָּנוּ (2 Sam 20:1, other forms Ezek 28:17, Prov 13:12, 15:17), compare וְעֶנְוָה־צֶּדֶק (Ps 45:5, other forms Mic 1:11, Ps 45:5, Prov 17:1). Despite the vocal *shewa* before the final *qames*, forms like נַחֲלָה act as members of category 4.

Other forms with *shewa* before a final *qames* also raise problems. Cases where the first word in a standard pair is a feminine form noun acting as an infinitive, as לְטָמְאָה־בָהּ (Lev 15:32, 18:20, 23, 22:8), וּלְדָבְקָה־בוֹ (Deut 11:22, 30:20, Jos 22:5) appear to have a closed penultimate syllable and typical final stress, like עֶנְוָה etc. They thus belong to category 4, so that conjunctive *dagesh* is not expected. However conjunctive *dagesh* is regularly used after imperative forms of apparently similar structure, as זָכְרָה־לִּי (Neh 5:19, similarly Neh 13:14, 22, 1 Chron 29:18) and שִׁמְעָה־לִּי (Job 32:10, similarly Job 34:16). Conjunctive *dagesh* is also used after two other forms in which the penultimate syllable would generally be considered closed: נַעַמְדָה־יָּחַד (Isa 50:8) and נַעֶזְבָה־נָּא (Neh 5:10). A vowel clearly was used between the last two root consonants of such forms in some traditions.[11] It is possible that the presence or absence of such a vowel was the factor which conditioned the use or non-

---

11. As is shown by the use of Waw before the last root consonant in imperative forms, as מָלוּכָה in Jud 9:8, and in נעמורה (Isa 50:8) in 1QIsa\u1d43. Cf. also יַעֲמֹרד In Cambridge University Library MS TS 16:96 (=P. E. Kahle, *MdW II*, MS J) Dan 11:14 (L יַעַמְדָוּ).

use of conjunctive *dagesh*. It is also possible that the conditioning factor was some other feature in which verbs characteristically differed from nouns.

Third person feminine singular perfect verb forms provide another case in which the status of *shewa* is uncertain. Such forms are followed by conjunctive *dagesh* in 74 cases, (excluding forms which are, or may be, f.s participles), as קָפְצָה פִּיהָ (Ps 107:42, Job 5:16). In another six cases, *dagesh* does not occur, as וּמָחֲתָה פִיהָ (Prov 30:20). As the examples indicate, there is no obvious reason for the 7% of exceptions. The *shewa* in such forms is quite often written as composite (as in Prov 30:20), and was unquestionably vocal at one time. In the present context, these forms would belong in category 4 if the *shewa* were silent. In this case conjunctive *dagesh* in the following word would be exceptional. In fact, however, the only forms in which a final *qames* which is typically stressed is preceded by a silent *shewa* are the noun and infinitive forms described above. Thus there is a possibility that the factor that governs the use of conjunctive *dagesh* is not the vocal or silent nature of the *shewa*, but some characteristic difference between verbs and nouns. The most obvious difference is the fact that, in nouns, stress on a final *qames* is not the result of a shift of stress from penultimate position, while in verb forms, it is.

If this difference is the conditioning factor, the description of conjunctive *dagesh* in words ending in *qames* can be simplified. Categories 2-3-4 can be replaced by the statement that conjunctive *dagesh* occurs after words in which the final *qames* was not originally stressed, not after those in which it was. Under this formulation, *waw* consecutive perfect forms are no longer exceptional, and there is no irregularity in the use of conjunctive *dagesh* after the superficially identical infinitive and imperative forms discussed above. The same applies to its use after סָאָה in the three cases of סָאָה־סֹלֶת (2 Kgs 7:1, 16, 18) in which the absence of conjunctive *dagesh* contrasts with its regular presence after imperative forms of the same structure, as in שְׁבָה־פֹּה (Rut 4:1 and 20 other cases). Exceptions to the standard pattern remain, of course, but under this simpler description the largest proportion is 8% in any category. Some of these 8% represent errors by the *naqdan* of L; others are phonologically conditioned. The remaining proportion of anomalies is small enough that it can be confidently stated that the phenomenon represented by conjunctive *dagesh* results automatically from close juncture in the situation described as a standard pair. It is not a Masoretic mystery, but a *sandhi* phenomenon. It is to be hoped that further study of a complete collection of cases of conjunctive *dagesh* will show that error or particular phonological conditioning accounts for the majority of anomalies, and so place this conclusion beyond the possibility of doubt.

THE BABYLONIAN MASORETIC TRADITION REFLECTED IN THE MSS OF THE TARGUM TO THE LATTER PROPHETS

Josep Ribera
University of Barcelona

1. Babylonian Puncutation.

To speak, nowdays, about Babylonian Punctuation it is necessary to take into account I. Yeivin's work,[1] which in a way we can consider as definitive, since it establishes the basic principles which govern this Masoretic Tradition. But we must point out, in spite of the exhaustiveness of this work, that it is only concerned with Biblical Hebrew texts and it mentions nothing of the Targumic versions.

Yeivin makes a distinction, as Kahle did,[2] between two main Babylonian Punctuation Systems: The Simple one (*Einfach*) and the Complicated one (*Kompliziert*). Within the Simple Babylonian System he classifies the MSS into three main groups: namely the ones belonging to Old, Middle and Recent Babylonian.

Schematically the Old Babylonian characteristics are, above all, the following: the original vocalic gutturals ʾ*alef*/ʿ*ayin* take no vowel or a full vowel; word ending final ʿ*ayin* sometimes takes *pataḥ*; copulative *waw* before a labial is vocalized with š*ewa* or is not punctuated; analogously before a consonant with š*ewa* either it is punctuated with ḥ*ireq* or has no sign; consonantal *yod* with š*ewa* is frequently punctuated with ḥ*ireq* and sometimes in a similar way *waw* with š*ewa* takes š*ureq*; mobile š*ewas* are marked with some frequency but quiescent š*ewas* are denoted with less frequency; within the word the auxiliary vowel is used, and sometimes the imperfect characteristic vowel is kept; vocalic interchanges are unusual; accents that are not marked on the stressed syllable are frequently indicated; diacritic signs, such

---

1. *The Hebrew Language Tradition as reflected in the Babylonian Vocalization*, Jerusalem 1985, 2 vols. (in Hebrew).
2. P. Kahle: "Die hebräischen Bibelhandschriften aus Babylonien", ZAW 46 (1928): 113-137.

as *dageš/rafe*, are sometimes indicated. Vocalization of MSS belonging to this category is more or less defective; sometimes another hand completes the defective part from the Babylonian System, although on occasions it vocalizes the text in Yemenite style.

As far as Middle Babylonian is concerned, this presents the following peculiarities: Generally the gutturals *'alef/'ayin* are punctuated with the full vowel, occasionally with *šewa*; copulative waw before labial is punctuated with *šewa* and before unvocalized consonants with *ḥireq*; the *yod-ḥireq* and *waw-šureq* phenomena usually disappear; almost each mobile *šewa* is indicated, but quiescent ones are scarcely denoted; within the word the auxiliary vowel practically disappears; in some MSS *ḥolem/ṣere, qameṣ/pataḥ*, and *pataḥ/šewa* are confused; diacritic *dageš/rafe* are almost never marked; accents are usually not found. Most of the MSS take full vocalization and, if one takes defective vocalization it is to a limited degree. Middle Babylonian is more similar to Tiberian than Old Babylonian and this is not because of its influence but because of the internal evolution of the Babylonian System. On the other hand, the vocalization characteristics of the Old Babylonian Complicated System are very similar to those of Middle Babylonian, besides the fact that it has a set of its own signs to mark, above all, closed syllables; the biggest difference between them is that in the Old Babylonian Complicated System there are many accents and quiescent *šewas*, and it also has signs belonging to the Tiberian System.

As far as MSS belonging to Recent Babylonian are concerned, it should be mentioned that they do not exclusively have Babylonian characteristics, but they usually have both Babylonian and Tiberian characteristics to a certain extent. All such MSS come from Yemen and they have to be studied within the Yemenite Tradition which we will speak of later.

Yeivin includes within each category a subdivision depending on the degree of purity in relation to the category the MS belongs to, and generally also depending on the degree to which these MSS have Babylonian characteristics. Thus, within Old Babylonian we find the V+, V, and V- classification; in Middle Babylonian IV, III+, III; in Recent Babylonian II+, II, I+, I.[3]

2. Biblical Targumic Text Vocalization.

The traditional Babylonian classification we have briefly described, along with its characteristics, is above all applicable to Biblical Hebrew and other Rabbinic Hebrew texts. But this tradition takes shape from the 7th to 9th centuries, spreading

---

3. Cf. Yeivin, op. cit., vol. I: 61-98.

from Babylon to other Jewish Communities that were then receiving the moral and juridical influence of the Gaons from Babylon; among those communities we must emphasize the importance of the Yemenite ones. Nevertheless, in that period in Babylonia the Jews were not only speakers of Aramaic, but many of their documents and scripts were written in that language as well. Thence Babylonian punctuation was also used to vocalize the official Targumim, because they got precisely in Babylonia their definitive structure and their official recognition. They are Onqelos' Targum to the Pentateuch and the Jonathan ben Uzziel's Targum to the Prophets. When Babylonian Masoretes -- because they spoke Aramaean, although in a dialectal form different from that of the official Targumim -- vocalized the Targumim, they doubtless projected in them a vocalization, in part or in all, that was alive and not either dead or purely literary, as happens with Biblical Hebrew. For this reason it is possible to suppose that the Babylonian vocalization in the Targumic texts is of a special quality, better, in our opinion, than that of the Hebrew text.

In fact, as we will see, in Yemenite MSS it is frequent to see that whilst the Hebrew text is tiberianized, the Targumic text often keeps the Babylonian vocalization, or at least it is more Babylonian than the Hebrew one.[4]

3. The Babylonian MSS of the Latter Prophets' Targum

I have centred the study on the Babylonian Masorah in the well-known MSS of Jonathan Ben Uzziel's Targum, and specially in the Latter Prophets. The results that we deduce from this are, however, in the same way applicable to the Former Prophets and in general to the official Targumim. Up to the present no full text of the Latter Prophets with Babylonian vocalization is known. There are only fragments of MSS of a varying length. Of the Targum of Isaiah we have only a third, and on the other hand, we have two thirds of that of Jeremiah, whilst of Ezekiel we have more or less a half. We also possess only a third of the Targumic text of the Minor Prophets. Most of the fragments have been published in my Doctoral Thesis.[5]

As the aim is, -- as I have recently done with the Targum of the Prophet Isaiah[6] -- to publish the Babylonian fragments, despite their unknown parts, as my teacher

---

4. Cf. A. Díez Macho: *Manuscritos hebreos y arameos de la Biblia* (Roma 1971): 24.

5. J. Ribera: *La Biblia Babilónica; Profetas Posteriores (Targum)*, Salamanca 1977.

6. J. Ribera: *Targum Jonatán de los Profetas Posteriores en tradición babilónica. Isaías*, Madrid 1988.

Prof. Díez Macho suggested to me, I have tried to look for a full Yemenite text in order to complete the Babylonian text. Why a Yemenite text? It is important to explain the value of Yemenite MSS, within the Oriental Babylonian Tradition in some detail.

4. The Yemenite Tradition of the Prophets' Targum.

We have just said that among the Yemenite Jewish communities, the Babylonian tradition of the Bible spread and crystalized in a special way, because of the moral authority exerted by the Babylonian Schools and the Gaons. Later on, in the 10th century, with the decay of those schools and the dawn of the Masoretic School in Tiberias, the Tiberian system gradually imposed itself.

With respect to MSS coming from Yemen, it is necessary to establish several categories: old MSS vocalized in the pure Babylonian System; MSS in some parts Babylonian and in others Tiberian; MSS exclusively Tiberian. But, besides, with respect to Yemenite MSS, we must distinguish between Hebrew text and Targumic text vocalization. Hebrew text tends to be vocalized in the Tiberian way sooner than the Targumic text, which is vocalized in that way only in part, never totally, except when the text is a recent one. So we very often find that while the Hebrew text is almost Tiberian, the Targumic one keeps close to the Middle Babylonian tradition (for instance MS Eb 51). The reasons for vocalizing the Hebrew and Aramaic texts in different ways are several. Whereas Babylonian Punctuation, based on the Aramaic language, was applied in the same way to Hebrew and Targumic texts, the Tiberian system was only applied to Hebrew texts and as a second function and only analogically it was deficiently adapted for Targum; as proof of this last fact we have the poor vocalization of the Targum found in most of the Occidental MSS with Tiberian punctuation. From that point of view the Oriental MSS from Yemen are very important as they offer us a very regular vocalization, which evidently has considerable repercussions on the grammatical text structure and in its comprehension.[7]

Thus, when we use Yemenite MSS for Targum although these have Tiberian elements, they are not to be considered as tiberianized in the real sense of the word. This can be proved with a list of Tiberian and Babylonian elements which are in this category of MSS.

---

7. Cf. Díez Macho, op. cit., pp. 25-28.

Tiberian elements:

1. Use of šureq with copulative waw before labials or consonants with sewa; but some examples according to Babylonian vocalization are also found.

2. Use of the ʾaktob form instead of Babylonian ʾiktob of the imperfect first person of peʿal.

3. Ṣere is substituted for šewa, closer to the Tiberian ḥaṭef-paṭaḥ in the Babylonian form ʾekateb in the first person singular of imperfect paʿel.

4. Generally, with some exceptions, gutturals, which in Babylonian are punctuated with full vowel, take šewa in Yemenite MSS, which is related to the Tiberian ḥaṭef.

5. The word כל, that in Babylonian is vocalized with ḥolem, in Yemenite is vocalized with qameṣ, equivalent to qameṣ-ḥaṭuf, although in Yemenite a complicated Babylonian sign is used to denote qameṣ-ḥaṭuf in particles such as qådam.

Babylonian elements:

1. Above all, the supralingual signs always are kept in Targum texts.

2. There is no sign for segol, pataḥ being found instead.

3. The compound šewas were unknown.

4. The lack of accent outside some atnaḥ, zaqef, and the normal use of sof-pasuq.

5. Normally there were no quiescent šewas; sporadic use of diacritic signs (dageš, rafe, maqqef, etc.) some vocalic interchanges (ṣere/ḥolem, qameṣ/pataḥ); the appearance, more or less frequently, of typically Babylonian forms.

Contrasting these elements and comparing them with the two main masoretic traditions, the Babylonian and the Tiberian ones, the Yemenite system seems a kind of mixture of both. This mixture, however, certainly constitutes a single, self contained entity that perhaps can be defined as a Yemenite Masoretic Tradition. That Yemenite scribes knew that is proved by the fact that in the Babylonian Tradition there is no record of the Targum of the Five Megillot, or of Hagiographa in general. But we find them vocalized in Yemenite style in MSS of these Jewish communities[8]

---

8. Cf. A. Van Der Heide: *The Yemenite Tradition of the Targum of Lamentations* (Leiden 1981): 37ff.

5. Evaluation of Babylonian MSS of Latter Prophets Targum.

For the study of the peculiarities of each MS I will direct you to the published introduction of my Doctoral Thesis. Now, I shall expose a synthesis of the results of that study.[9]

Describing the most important characteristics, above all the ones belonging to MSS of Old and Middle Babylonian, they show us that the differential limits of each category as regards its vocalization of the Targumic text are not determinant at all. Yet, one of the consequences of this, because of the individual peculiarities of each MSS, is that the Babylonian System is more a kind of systematization than a complete system imposed on us, and each MS presents its own aspects that are not of the assigned group. For instance, MS Eb 52, which, because of its main characteristics, belongs to Middle Babylonian, uses the auxiliary vowel very frequently, which is a particular characteristic of Old Babylonian. Other MSS of Middle Babylonian, such as Eb 71 or Eb 111 have a large number of accents, which is also a characteristic of Old Babylonian; besides Eb 111 marks, as in Old Babylonian, the quiescent šewas. Sometimes we find MSS of the Old Babylonian group, for instance Eb 113, which are almost fully vocalized, as MSS in the Middle Babylonian group are. Neither is it to be forgotten that several old MSS, which at first were defective, when copied anew were completed with full vocalization, in the Babylonian System or in the Yemenite one, or even in the Tiberian one.

Thence one can conclude:

1. The Phonetics of the Babylonian Masorah with respect to Hebrew text and Aramaic Targum are very similar. Due to the influence of Aramaic as a living language on Hebrew as only a literary language, we believe that they are more characteristic of Aramaic than of Hebrew.

2. The classification of the MSS with Babylonian masorah into three kinds, proposed by I. Yeivin (OB, MB, RB), applied to Hebrew texts can be used for Targumic texts, but with some exceptions. There is, above all, in Aramaic the tendency to vocalize the gutturals more than in Hebrew; the more frequent use of the auxiliary vowel and very often the lack, in Aramaic, of a second Tiberian or Yemenite hand that corrects the Babylonian text. Besides, there are MSS that in the Targum are plainly of a superior category to the Hebrew (cf. Eb 29, Eb 86, Eb 96, Kb 8).

---

9. J. Ribera: *Targum Babilónico a los Profetas* (Barcelona 1973): (75)-(78) (manuscript); *Targum Jonatán* ... pp. 33-34.

3. It seems that subdivisions from V to I made by Yeivin, are not appropriate for Aramaic. The phonetic variations of Targum that appear among the MSS of the same kind are peculiar to each MS, which are not found in the subdivisions to which it belongs. Eb 24, for example, has characteristics corresponding to OB and to MB.

4. We must also take into account, when cataloguing MSS, examples, for instance, that at first were defective and vocalized in the OB category and were then completed by a second Tiberian or Yemenite-Tiberian hand, so they have been catalogued incorrectly in the RB category; for example Eb 25.

5. It could also be said that Babylonian MSS have suffered some influence of the Old Palestinian vocalization. This could explain the šewa/pataḥ confusion in MS Eb 24.

6. As a result of everything that has been said, it may be deduced that there are common peculiarities to the three classifications that we have synthesized (OB, MB, OCB), which are really useful to define the Babylonian System clearly in comparison with the Palestinian and Tiberian Systems, and that the Babylonian vocalization that we find in the MSS of the Official Targumim has a special place for this study.

A STUDY OF וַיֹּאמֶר IN THE MASORA FINALIS

Milton Weinberg
Monsey, New York

The usual vocalization of the *qal* future third person singular with *waw* conversive of "and he said" is with *segol* under *mem*, and with penultimate stress, i.e., מלעיל, viz., וַיֹּאמֶר.[1] However, in pausal form the vocalization changes from *segol* to *patah* under *mem*, and the stress shifts to the ultimate, i.e., מלרע, viz., וַיֹּאמַר.

There is a note in the masora finalis (MF) of the editio princeps of the Rabbinic Bible[2] (s. מערכת אות האלף, i.e., the alphabetical listings under the letter אלף) with a heading which states:

ויאמר חד מן צ״א וסימנהון ...
(With regard to the form) וַיֹּאמֶר, it is one of
(א״צ) 91 (חד מן) instances, and the
references are (וסימנהון)...

There follows a list of catchwords and phrases which identify the verses.[3] By

---

1. C.D. Ginsburg in *The Massorah*, Reprinted by KTAV Publishing House, New York, 1976, vol. 4, p. 103, 842, points out there are 1,951 occurrences of וַיֹּאמֶר in The Bible.

2. Biblia Rabbinica, A Reprint of the 1525 Venice Edition, Makor Pub. Ltd., Jerusalem, 1972.

3. Gen 14:19; 15:8; 16:8; 18:3, 23, 27, 29; 19:7; 20:4, 24:12, 34; 27:36; 28:13, 17; 30:28; 33:5; 37:30; 43:29; 47:30; 48:9, 15; Exod 2:14; 5:22; 32:31, 5; 33:14, 18; Num 11:27, 28; 21:2; 23:12, 7, 18; 24:3, 15, 23, 20, 21; Deut 33:2, 7; Jos 7:20; Judg 6:18; 8:19; 11:30; 13:8; 15:18; 16:28; 20:4; 1 Sam 3:18; 7:12; 22:9, 14; 2 Sam 15:21; 3:33; 19:27; 20:20; 22:2; 23:15; 1 Kgs 1:29; 8:23; 17:10, 11, 20, 21; 18:36; 2 Kgs 1:8; 2:14; 6:17, 18, 20; 7:2, 19; 13:14; 19:15; Isa 38:3; Amos 1:2; Jonah 3:4; 4:2; Zech 1:10, 12; l Chron 11:17; 2 Chron 6:14; 20:6; 14:10; Ps 18:2; Dan 9:22; 8:16; Ruth 2:6; Job 1:14, 16, 17, 18.

noting ..צ״א, the masora seeks to safeguard the minority occurrences of this verb vocalized with *pataḥ* and stressed ultimate, in contrast to the 1,951 cases in which it is with segol and stressed penultimate.

However, the accompanying list of catchwords and phrases recorded in the MF numbers 92 verses, not 91 as stated in the heading. Ginsburg[4] points out this error, and calls attention to the extraneous verse (i.e., listing #70) where the catch-word and phrase are: וַיִּתְפַּלֵּל וַיְהִי כְּבוֹאָם שֹׁמְרוֹן.[5] He notes that the phrase וַיְהִי כְּבוֹאָם שֹׁמְרוֹן, at 2 Kgs 6:20, is followed by וַיֹּאמֶר. It plainly does not fit the rubric heading (..וַיֹּאמֶר הַד מִן צ״א). Furthermore, Ginsburg remarks that the catchword, וַיִּתְפַּלֵּל, itself does not appear in 2 Kgs 6:20. וַיִּתְפַּלֵּל does occur in the two listings immediately preceding #70, i.e., 2 Kgs 6:17, 18. Confusion on the part of the scribe may have led to this double error.

There are 4 other errors in this masora finalis list, two of which were noted by Ginsburg:

(1) In listing #31 וְרִפֶן, given as the catchword followed by וַיֹּאמֶר הֲלֹא אֶת אֲשֶׁר, is incorrect. This phrase is found at Num 23:12; however, וְרִפֶן does not occur there. The verse at Num 23:12 reads ... וַיַּעַן וַיֹּאמֶר הֲלֹא אֵת אֲשֶׁר. It would seem that carelessness on the part of the scribe caused the erroneous וְרִפֶן to appear in the masoretic list.

(2) In listing #83, אֲבוֹתֵינוּ is the catchword followed by a phrase in which the abbreviation יש׳ (יִשְׂרָאֵל) is mistakenly recorded. The citation should read וַיֹּאמֶר יְיָ׳ אֱלֹהֵי אֲבוֹתֵינוּ and not the given יש׳ אלהי ירי ויאמר. In this case, the scribe may have been influenced by the previous listing, #82, (2 Chron 6:14) in which יש׳ appears, viz., אֵין כָּמוֹךָ   וַיֹּאמֶר יְיָ׳ אֱלֹהֵי יש׳ דר״ה.

The two errors in the MF list which Ginsburg did not indicate in his remarks are:

(1) Listing #50 (1 Sam 7:12): the phrase should be וַיִּקַּח שְׁמוּאֵל אֶבֶן. However, לוֹ was added so that עַד הֵנָּה   וַיִּקַּח לוֹ שְׁמוּאֵל אֶבֶן became erroneously recorded in the masora finalis. Was the scribe influenced by a previous citation, viz., listing #49 (1 Sam 3:18, אֵת וַיַּגֶּד-לוֹ שְׁמוּאֵל   כחד) where לוֹ occurs?

---

4. Op. cit.

5. Ginsburg mistakenly refers to this citation as "...the seventeenth instance..." rather than the seventieth.

(2) Listing #63 (1 Kgs 17:20) should read וַיִּקְרָא אֶל־יי' מִתְגּוֹרֵר וַיִּתְפַּלֵּל אֶל יי' וַיֹּאמֶר instead of וַיֹּאמֶר. מִתְגּוֹרֵר וַיִּתְפַּלֵּל is not found at all in 1 Kgs 17:20.

At the conclusion of this long list of catchwords and phrases in the masora finalis, there is this note

... וכל ויען ויוסף דאיוב דכו'

And in every instance (וכל) of ויען and
ויוסף in Job (דאיוב), it is written this way
(דכו' = דכותיה).

This same masoretic remark - וכל ויען ויוסף דאיוב דכו' - is also found in the masora parva in B19a,[6] The Aleppo Codex,[7] and The Cairo Codex.[8]

This concluding comment of the MF is difficult to understand. To what does it refer? What was the purpose of the masoretes in making such a remark? Reading it, one might think that דכו' (...it is written this way) refers to ויאמר appearing in Job together with ויען(ו)/סף(ו) having the same vocalization and stress as the "91" instances recorded in the MF (viz., וַיֹּאמֶר). But if that is the case, why were these instances not included along with the other occurrences of וַיֹּאמֶר in the masora finalis list? Why should there be a separate note concerning these occurrences in Job?

In the citations of וַיֹּאמֶר listed in the MF, the last 4 mentioned (#89, 90, 91, 92) all appear in the first chapter of Job, viz., verses 14, 16, 17, and 18 respectively; however, none of them contains the verbs ויען or ויסף(ו). Examining וַיֹּאמֶר in a concordance,[9] a total of 36 instances in Job were found: the 4 already cited in the masora finalis, and 32 others which were not listed. Thus, it would appear that the

---

6. Gen 14:19 in Pentateuch. Prophets and Hagiographa, Codex Leningrad B19a, Facsimile Edition, v.1: 18, Makor Publishing, Jerusalem, 1972.

7. Judg 20:4, The Aleppo Codex, Magnes Press, Jerusalem, 1976.

8. El Codice De Profetas De El Cairo, ed. F. Perez Castro et al, v.1, Instituto Arias Montano, Madrid, 1980. At Jos 7:20 (p. 41), a footnote states that the comment, וכל ויען ויוסף דאיוב דכו', is found in the Cairo Codex at Jud 11:30, 15:18, 20:4, 1 Sam 3:18, 22:14; 2 Sam 15:21, 19:27, 20:20; 1 Kgs 8:23, 17:10, 18:36; 2 Kgs 2:14, 6:17, 18, 13:14; Zech 1:10,12; i.e., a total of 17 times.

9. S. Mandelkern, Concordance of the Old Testament (Schocken, Tel Aviv, 1962): 126; see also, Ginsburg, Op. cit.

MF comment, ׳וכל ויען ויוסף דאיוב דכו, refers to these 32 instances of ויאמר in Job in which ויען appears in 29 verses;[10] and ויסף(ו) in 3 verses.[11]

Ginsburg[12] translates the comment ׳וכל ויען ויוסף דאיוב דכו as follows:

"וַיֹּאמֶר occurs ninety-one times...and whenever it is preceded by וַיַּעַן or וַיֹּסֶף in Job it is likewise so..."

ויען/וי(ו)סף do precede ויאמר in these 32 verses, but the fact that they do is not readily evident from the masoretic comment itself. וכל ויען ויוסף דאיוב דכו׳ gives no hint with regard to the order of the words in the verses. One has to examine the verses to determine this pattern. Moreover, in the MF list of the "91", there are 14 other instances of וַיַּעַן[13] and 1 of וַיֹּסֶף[14] which occur in the same verse with וַיֹּאמֶר. In each of these 15 instances (in biblical books other than Job), ויען/וי(ו)סף also precede ויאמר. Thus, the fact that ויען/וי(ו)סף comes before ויאמר is not unique to Job. As it appears in the MF of the *editio princeps*, to what does the comment ׳וכל ויען ויוסף דאיוב דכו refer? What was its purpose? Why should these 32 instances warrant special attention?

The answer may be found in the masora finalis of the 3rd Edition of the Rabbinic Bible (s., מערכת אות האלף),[15] There, the editor of that edition of *Biblia Rabbinica* made the following changes and corrections:

(1) The heading states simply

וַיֹּאמֶר צ״א וסימנהון...

...וַיֹּאמֶר occurs 91 times, and the references are...[16]

---

10. 1:7,9; 2:2,4; 3:2; 4:1; 6:1; 8:1; 9:1; 11:1; 12:1; 15:1; 16:1; 18:1; 19:1; 20:1; 21:1; 22:1; 23:1; 25:1; 26:1; 32:6; 34:1; 35:1; 38:1; 40:1, 3, 6; 42:1.

11. 27:1; 29:1; 36:1.

12. *Op. cit.*

13. Gen 18:27; Num 11:28, 23:12; Jos 7:20; Judg 20:4; 1 Sam 22:9, 14; 2 Sam 15:21, 20:20; 2 Kgs 7:2, 19; Zech 1:10, 12; Ruth 2:6.

14. Gen 18:29

15. *Biblia Rabbinica*, Venice, Bomberg, 1546-48; also see *Biblia Rabbinica*, ed. J. Buxtorf, 1619; *Miqraoth Gedoloth*, Pardes Publishing House, Inc., N.Y., 1951.

16. Gen 14:19; 15:8; 16:8; 18:3, 23, 27, 29; 19:7; 20:4, 24:12; 24:34; 27:36; 28:13, 17; 30:28; 33:5; 37:30; 43:29; 47:30; 48:9, 15; Exod 2:14; 5:22; 32:31, 5; 33:14, 18; Num 11:27, 28; 21:2; 23:12, 7, 18; 24:3, 15, 23, 20, 21; Deut 33:2, 7; Jos 7:20; Judg 6:18; 8:19; 11:30; 13:8; 15:18; 16:28; 20:4; 1 Sam 3:18; 7:12; 22:9, 14; 2 Sam 15:21; 3:33; 19:27;

(2) The heading states "91" (צ״א), and 91 verses (not 92 as in the 2nd Edition) are listed, correctly corresponding with the rubric heading. The erroneous verse found in the masora finalis of the *editio princeps* (2 Kgs 6:20, i.e., listing #70) is deleted in the 3rd Edition. However, the other errors in the masora finalis which were discussed above remain uncorrected.

(3) Added to the conclusion of the list of catchwords and phrases is the remark אבל הם כולם מלעיל so that the comment at the end of the MF in the 3rd Edition now reads:

וכל ויען ויוסף דאיוב דכו׳
אבל הם כולם מלעיל

And in every instance of ויען and ויוסף in Job, it is written this way, but they are all stressed penultimate (מלעיל, אבל הם כולם), viz., (וַיֹּאמֶר).

Appearing by itself, as it does in the *editio princeps*, וכל ויען ויוסף דאיוב דכו׳ poses questions and problems. It would seem that the editor of the 3rd Edition, upon reviewing this note in the MF, added the phrase אבל הם כולם מלעיל, to shed light on the intent of the original comment. This revised remark now serves as a *caveat* to indicate that there are instances in which ויען/ויוסף occur in Job together with ויאמר and are "...written this way..." (i.e., pausal and with *pataḥ*); and although one might expect them to be stressed מלרע (ultimate, as are the "91" others on the list), these instances in Job are "all" מלעיל (penultimate). The editor of the 3rd Edition thought that וכל ויען ויוסף דאיוב דכו׳, appearing alone in the MF of the *editio princeps*, did not convey this intent; therefore, there was the need for the additional clarification: אבל הם כולם מלעיל.

Is אבל הם כולם מלעיל a masoretic comment? Had the phrase been omitted inadvertently from the 2nd Edition through a scribal or printing error? Or was it written by the editor of the 3rd Edition in order to correct what may have appeared to be a misleading and difficult remark in the MF? These questions remain to be answered in another study. אבל הם כולם מלעיל is not found in the B19a or

---

20:20; 22:2; 23:15; 1 Kgs 1:29; 8:23; 17:10, 11, 20, 21; 18:36; 2 Kgs 1:8; 2:14; 6:17, 18; 7:2, 19; 13:14; 19:15; Isa 38:3; Amos 1:2, Jonah 3:4; 4:2; Zech 1:10, 12; 1Chron 11:17; 2 Chron 6:14; 20:6; 14:10; Ps 18:2; Dan 9:22; 8:16; Ruth 2:6; Job 1:14, 16, 17, 18.

Aleppo codices; nor is there any reference to it in the Cairo Codex. It is also of interest to note, that in all of Ginsburg's comment on ויאמר, he does not mention אבל הם כולם מלעיל although it was known to Kimḥi, Levita, Minḥat Shai, and Frensdorff among others.

Minḥat Shai, commenting on [וַיַּ֣עַן] at Job 3:2, states:

ויען איוב ויאמר. בפתח גדול ומלעיל וכן
במסורת חשיב צ״א פתחין ומלרע וכל ויען
ויוסף דאיוב דכוותא אבל הם כולם מלעיל
וכן במכלול דף קי״ג ובספר הבחור
מאמר ב׳ עיקר ו׳

In the verse וַיִּאָמַ֔ר, וַיַּ֣עַן אִיּוֹב֙ וַיֹּאמַ֔ר is vocalized with *pataḥ*, but with penultimate stress. And the masora reckoned 91 instances of ויאמר vocalized with *pataḥ* and accented on the ultimate...

Minḥat Shai emphasized that at Job 3:2 [וַיֹּאמַ֔ר] is to be vocalized with פתח גדול, (*pataḥ*) but stressed penultimate (ומלעיל). He uses the term פתח גדול intentionally in order to assure that the vocalization would not be פתח קטן (i.e., *segol*,[17] the expected vocalization of ויאמר with penultimate stress). Noting the 91 instances in the masora of ויאמר vocalized with *pataḥ* (פתחין), and accented מלרע (וַיֹּאמַ֔ר), Minḥat Shai quotes the revised remark found in the MF of the 3rd Edition, וכל ויען ויוסף דאיוב דכוותא אבל הם כולם מלעיל and concludes by referring to the works of David Kimḥi and Elijah Levita to support the view that these instances are stressed penultimate.

...And similarly in (Kimḥi's) *Mikhlol*, p. 113
(וכן במכלול דף קי״ג),[18] and in (Levita's) *Sefer Habaḥur*, article 2, principle 6 (ובספר הבחור
מאמר ב׳ עיקר ו׳)[19]

In *Sefer Habaḥur*, Levita remarks

וַיֹּאמַר...ומלרע חוץ מן וַיַּעַן אִיּוֹב וַיֹּאמַר

---

17. See E. Levita's *The Massoreth Hamassoreth*, p. 131-32, translated by C.D. Ginsburg, reprinted by KTAV Publishing, New York, 1968, for a discussion of these vowels.

18. ספר מכלול, ed. Isaac ben Aharon Rittenberg, p. 85a, Lycke, 1842.

19. ספר הבחור, Elijah ben Asher, the Levite, article 2, p. 17a, Berlin, 1767.

(איוב ג) וחבריו כלם מלעיל
וַיַּעַן אִיוֹב וַיֹּאמַר מלרע is ...וַיֹּאמֶר[except for
(Job 3) and its companions (וחבריו);
they are all מלעיל (כלם) (penultimate).

Of the 32 occurrences of ויען/וי(ו)סף together with וַיֹּאמַר in Job, 27 are with *silluq* [24 with וַיַּעַן and 3 with וַיֹּ(ו)סֶף]. There is a difference of opinion in regard to the placement of *silluq* in these 27 instances. There are two distinct traditions: in the 2nd and 3rd Editions of *Biblia Rabbinica*, the *silluq* is placed under *yod*[20] with the stress מלעיל (the position with which Kimḥi, Levita, and Minḥat Shai agreed); while at the same 27 occurrences in the B19a and Aleppo codices the *silluq* is under *mem* with the stress מלרע.

In the light of a difference of opinion over the placement of the *silluq*, the comment צ״א וכל ויען ויוסף דאיוב דכו׳ found at the MP in B19a (Gen 14:19) and Aleppo (Judg 20:4) may now be better understood. This note may have been a *caveat* on the part of a school of masoretes made in order <u>to prevent</u> the placement of the *silluq* under *yod* (i.e., with penultimate stress) in these instances of ויאמר in Job:

> There are 91 instances of ויאמר (with *pataḥ* and stressed ultimate) and in every instance of ויען/ויוסף in Job (i.e., the 27 with *silluq*) it is written this way (like the "91" with *pataḥ* and stressed ultimate).

In the B19a and Aleppo codices there is consistency between the masora parva and the texts: in the 27 instances the *silluq* is under *mem* (וַיֹּאמַר). Perhaps somehow, this masoretic comment became part of the MF in the *editio princeps*. As it has been shown in this study, placed there, the comment is misleading. In that very edition of the printed bible, in these same 27 cases, the *silluq* appears under *yod* (וַיֹּאמֶר). There was the need to correct this inconsistency, and clarify the comment by adding the phrase אבל הם כולם מלעיל found in MF in the 3rd Edition.

As to the remaining 5 occurrences of וַיֹּאמֶר in Job, unlike the matter of *silluq*, there is no difference of opinion within the sources concerning accentuation. There is

---

20. Job 3:2, 4:1, 6:1, 8:1, 9:1; 11:1; 12:1; 15:1; 16:1; 18:1; 19:1; 20:1; 21:1; 22:1; 23:1, 25:1; 26:1; 27:1; 29:1; 34:1; 35:1; 36:1; 38:1; 40:1, 3, 6; 42:1.

agreement that the accent of וַיֹּאמֶר] in each of these 5 instances is: *oleh veyored* once, and *etnaḥ* and *zaqef qaton* twice each,[21] i.e., stressed מלרע. In the codices, וכל ("And in every instance...") also refers to these 5 instances of וַיֹּאמֶר where the stress is ultimate.

But in the MF of the 3rd Edition, with regard to these 5 occurrences, the use of the remark אבל הם כולם מלעיל now raises questions. Does the comment "all" (כולם) include these 5 cases? Is the intent of אבל הם כולם מלעיל to indicate that although the stress in these 5 instances is ultimate, they are like the 27 other instances, i.e., to be read "as if" they were penultimate? That would be most unusual, unlikely, and unacceptable. Therefore, the remark "all" with regard to these 5 instances is misleading. It does not point to "all" 32 instances of ויען/ויוסף found in Job with וַיֹּאמֶר, but only "all" of those 27 instances which have *silluq* under *yod*, i.e., the parallel passages (וחברירן) to which Levita, Kimḥi, and Minḥat Shai refer in commenting on וַיֹּאמֶר] at Job 3:2. Was the term וחברירן omitted from the comment אבל הם כולם מלעיל inadvertently? Or was it understood without the need to make it explicit? And if אבל הם כולם מלעיל refers only to the 27 occurrences of וַיֹּאמֶר] in Job, why weren't these 5 instances of וַיֹּאמֶר included in the MF list with all the other instances of וַיֹּאמֶר?

Ginsburg's remark[22] that " וַיַּעַן] וַיֹּסֶף]... correctly indicates" the 27 instances stressed penultimate, and the 5 stressed ultimate is puzzling. The comment, וכל ויען ויוסף דאיוב דכו', which appears in the masora parva of codices such as B19a and Aleppo, and in the masora finalis of the *editio princeps* does not give such an indication, and is not at all that obvious. Rather, the masoretic comment is unclear and requires further explanation.

A number of questions surrounding this masoretic note have yet to be resolved. However it came to be formulated, the concluding note in the masora finalis of the 3rd Edition of the *Biblia Rabbinica* seeks to preserve those exceptional cases of וַיֹּאמֶר which, according to one masoretic tradition, are pausal, written with *pataḥ* under *mem*, but accented מלעיל (וַיֹּאמֶר]). This is in contrast to majority of instances in which it is מלרע (וַיֹּאמֶר]).

---

21. 1:7 (*qaton*), 9 (*etnaḥ*); 2:2 (*qaton*), 4 (*etnaḥ*); 32:6 (*oleh veyored*).
22. *Op. cit.*

וַיֹּאמֶר *in the Masora Finalis* / 119

The total number of instances of our form with *pataḥ* under *mem* in the Bible is 123. 91 are listed in the masora finalis, and 32 in Job together with the ויען/ויוסף.

OBSERVATIONS ON THE OLD ACCUSATIVE ENDING IN MASORETIC HEBREW

P. C. H. Wernberg-Møller
Oxford University

The system of orthography and vocalization employed in biblical MSS reflects an advanced stage in the history of biblical Hebrew; and the simplified scribal conventions often obscure original linguistic features which, as suggested by diachronic and comparative study of Hebrew as a member of the Semitic family of languages, were present in the language before the process of simplification and levelling had been completed. One such feature, viz. the final, unstressed /a/ attached to some place names, appellatives and adverbs, is the subject of this paper.

Scribal conventions are, of course in terms of linguistic history relatively late, but, as I shall attempt to suggest below, the final, unstressed /a/ arose out of separate phonological and morphological developments which resulted in the emergence of a single morpheme /-a/ already in pre-biblical times; and eventually even this single morpheme lost its function, although biblical Hebrew contains evidence of it, both as posessing a directional force, and fulfilling a grammatical function at clause level.[1]

---

1. That eventually not only the directional /a/, but also the formally identical accusative ending lost its original function can be seen e.g. in cases where the accusatives are construed with prepositions, as e.g. לִישְׁעָתָה (Ps 80:3, בַּצְרָתָה Ps 120:1) etc., cf. F. Böttcher, *Ausführliches Lehrbuch der Hebräischen Sprache*, I (1866), para 843 (p. 630f.). J. Ohlshausen, in order to explain the improper use of the ה locale ending which he, like other philologists of his generation, identified with the accusative case ending, developed a theory according to which the ה locale was reintroduced into Hebrew after the general disappearance of the case endings, and at a time when prepositions were no longer felt to require the genitive in Hebrew (see his *Lehrbuch der hebräischen Sprache* [1861]:245ff.). This ingenious theory can now be regarded as obsolete in view of the Ugaritic evidence. Equally outdated is Ohlshausen's theory that a feminine form was originally intended in those cases where the ending /a/ appears 'meaningless'. The unsatisfactory nature of this theory may be seen e.g. in his

However, in order to begin to understand the functions of this morpheme it is necessary to consider its origins and to distinguish between the originally consonantal and originally vocalic morpheme.

Before 1928 (the year of the discovery of the Ras Shamra tablets) scholars generally agreed on the close connection between the ה locale and the old Semitic accusative ending.[2] There was, however, one notable voice of dissent, viz. that of Chr.

---

explanation of בְּעֵרָה תַּנּוּר כְּמוֹ in Hos 7:4 (op. cit. p. 253) where בְּעֵרָה cannot have been intended as a feminine form as תַּנּוּר is masculine: בְּעֵרָה is better described as a masculine accusative form ('like an oven in a state of burning'). For this type of construction in Arabic *(naṣb al-ḥal* according to the Arabic grammarians) see e.g. W. Wright, *A Grammar of the Arabic Language*, II (1875):122ff. and W. Fischer (ed.) *Grundriss der arabischen Philologie*, I (1982):70f. Cf. n. 39 and n. 40 below for additional instances of an original accusative form mistakenly being described as a feminine form.

2. For classical statements about the identity of the ה locale and the accusative ending see J. Barth in *Zeitschrift der deutschen morgenländischen Gesellschaft* 53 (1899):596; F. Böttcher, op. cit., pp. 623-32; B. Stade, *Lehrbuch der hebräischen Grammatik* (1897):202f. For the theory that the consonantal demonstrative element /ha/ is the original form of the common Semitic accusative ending, see A. Dillmann, *Ethiopic Grammar* (1907), para. 143 and F. W. M. Philippi, *Wesen und Ursprung des Status Constructus im Hebräischen* (1871):174ff. The suffix /ha/ is used in Ethiopic as an accusative marker with proper names, and in Ugaritic as a directional indicator. That the common accusative ending developed from this demonstrative suffix is not impossible in view of the fact that, in Indo-European languages, case endings can be seen to have arisen from adverbs and particles added to noun stems (for a brief statement about this matter, see e.e. Ph. Baldi, in B. Comrie [ed.] *The World's Major Languages* [1987]:53). What is interesting about Ugaritic in this connection is that it has preserved the full consonantal suffix with the original directional function together with the full common Semitic case system, whereas in Hebrew the two endings are identical. Without the Ugaritic evidence we should never have known the true background of the Hebrew ה locale. It is conceivable, of course, that what now appears in MT as a *mater lectionis* was (without the final vowel) pronounced with a light breathing already in Ugaritic (cf. C. Gordon, *Ugaritic Grammar* [1967]:112). However, as the demonstrative particle /ha/ -- used either as a prefix or a suffix -- is wide-spread, and considering the generally archaic nature of Ugaritic with regard to the preservation of final vowels, the suffix in Ugaritic (and originally in Hebrew also) is likely to have ended in a vowel which in Hebrew was dropped at some stage, exposing the weakly articulated /h/ -- at the end of a final unstressed syllable -- and causing its disappearance. That a different

Sarauw[3] who argued that there was no etymological connection between these two speech elements; and although some details in Sarauw's argument are open to criticism, and, as we can now see, in need of correction, his basic assumption has proved to be correct, in the sense that the two suffixes can now be seen to have been different originally although in Hebrew they merged into one and the same at an early stage.[4]

The Ugaritic evidence of the enclitic /h/ -- presumably the demonstrative suffix /ha/ -- functioning in some passages, though not in all, as indicating movement and direction in space and time, suggests that in Hebrew also the suffix was *originally* consonantal. However, as in biblical Hebrew the ending is always vocalic, and not

---

stress pattern is required for the preservation of /h/ at the end of a word can be seen in the feminine suffix (סוּסָה *sūsā́ha). The preservation of a final vowel in an unstressed position is a very remarkable and unusual feature in Hebrew. The explanation lies in the demonstrative suffix being attached to a fully formed, morphemic unit whose stress pattern could not be changed through the addition of a further suffix, and the main stress could therefore not be on the connecting vowel, hence *sifrā́ha סִפְרָה, but *yamī́maha יָמִימָה. Cf. n. 17 below.

3. "Der hebräische Lokativ" in *Zeitschrift für Assyriologie*, 20 (1907):183-189. For a well-documented article on the ה locale in the light of Canaanite-Ugaritic and Akkadian, see E. A. Speiser, *Oriental and Biblical Studies* (Collected Writings of E. A. Speiser, edd. Finkelstein and Greenberg), 1967:494ff. Speiser, taking his clue from the directional sense of the enclitic /h/ in Ugaritic, separates the ה locale from the common Semitic accusative ending, but -- I think mistakenly -- disregards the possibility that the unstressed /a/ in Hebrew may in some cases be the accusative ending. See n. 31 below.

4. Sarauw (art. cit., p. 184), with most scholars, recognized the ending /a/ as a survival of the locative in e.g. לַיְלָה. This view has been indirectly confirmed by the discovery of /h/ as a *consonantal* suffix in Ugaritic (distinct from the vocalic suffix /a/), for it would be absurd to suggest that the ה locale, as an originally *consonantal* ending, occurs in a word like לַיְלָה. However, Sarauw distinguishes rather too sharply between the locative and the accusative. The distinction to be made is between the accusative used as a locative on the one hand, and the suffix /h/ (probably /aha/) used directionally, on the other. The former is a linguistic feature common to all the Semitic languages, the latter is a specifically NW Semitic (and Ethiopic) function of a widespread Semitic speech element.

always functioning spatially and kinetically, the suffix might well, in a number of instances, be the accusative case ending, common to all the Semitic languages and functioning in a great variety of ways. A task -- perhaps an impossible one -- for the linguistic historian of Hebrew might be to attempt to determine to what extent the two originally separate endings could be distinguished. Although a complete separation of the (originally consonantal) ה locale occurrences from the survivals of the (originally vocalic) case ending is beyond the capabilities of even the most ingenious philologist, it is worth pointing out that, due to the vocalic structure of the suffix in MT, the burden of proof lies with those who deny the possibility that the accusative case ending has survived in masoretic Hebrew. In Ugaritic the position seems clear: the enclitic /h/ and the vocalic accusative case ending are clearly distinguished, but unfortunately this fact does not help us very much. Because of the dual background of the Hebrew vocalic suffix, and also because of inner-Hebrew developments which, as far as we can see, did not occur in Ugaritic, the Ugaritic evidence is of little more than etymological importance, as it proves nothing more than the originally separate existence of the two morphemes.[5] In Ugaritic the *consonantal* suffix, and in Hebrew the corresponding *vocalic* suffix are both attached to nouns as a marker of direction in time and space; although the Ugaritic evidence is scant and is obscured by a few occurrences in which the suffix appears to have some other function,[6] the parallel between Ugaritic and Hebrew is strengthened by a striking overlap in vocabulary, the common words for 'earth' and 'heaven' occurring in both languages with their respective suffixes clearly indicating movement and direction in space. In the case of אֶרֶץ, however, the suffix is not always directional,

---

5. In fact it could be said that the Ugaritic evidence, although proving the originally consonantal nature of the ה locale and the directional force of the suffix in NW Semitic, poses a serious problem for Hebrew philologists because of the loss in Hebrew of linguistic distinctions which must at some stage have been features of the language, and because of the uncertainty flowing from this development as to the degree to which Ugaritic and Hebrew are, in fact, comparable. Cf. n. 6 below.

6. Cf. J. Aistleitner, *Wörterbuch der Ugaritischen Sprache* (1963):84 (nos. 805, 806, 807). S. Segert, *A Basic Grammar of the Ugaritic Language* (1984), para. 58.2 is uncertain about the precise function of the enclitic /h/ in Ugaritic. S. Moscati (ed.), *An Introduction to the Comparative Grammar of the Semitic Languages* (1964), para. 12.67, avoids the term ה locale, speaks of the Hebrew ending -â as denoting motion towards a place and makes no mention of the Ugaritic evidence. Cf. n. 13 below.

but is better taken as an accusative form of אֶרֶץ;[7] and the stationary function of the suffix /a/ in Hebrew has an equivalent in Ugaritic, where the enclitic /h/ may be used for that purpose,[8] although the accusative case appears to have been more commonly used to express that function.[9] In fact, on the basis of the Ugaritic evidence, one could conclude that originally the ה locale was a local-terminative or temporal-terminative ending, and the accusative was used as a locative to express 'place where', in the rather loose way characteristic of the circumstantial or adverbial accusative (that may well tie up with the fact that, in Hebrew, words like מִזְרָחָה אַרְצָה, יָמָּה, בַּיְמָה,, as locatives are used without the definite article, although admittedly there is no strict consistency here, cf. e.g. הַמִּזְבֵּחָה 'on the altar').[10] In

---

7. See *Gesenius' Hebrew Grammar*, ed. Kautzsch (1910), para. 90f. for some examples, אַרְצָה being one of them, in which the accusative ending has been preserved in object constructions; cf. nn. 31, 39, 40, 41, 42 below for further instances of this phenomenon which can be observed both in prose and in poetry.

8. J. C. L. Gibson, *Canaanite Myths and Legends* (1978):123 (text 2₁₁) is right in implying in his translation that the suffix /h/ is used locatively in šdmth.

9. Cf. e.g. tškn šd .... pʾat mdbr 'They settled on the field .... on the fringe of the wilderness'(Gibson, op. cit., p. 87, 11. 192-3) and see n.25 below.

10. I would include שָׁכַב אַרְצָה (2 Sam 12:16) here, as an example of the accusative functioning as a locative, *pace* J. Hoftijzer, *A Search for Method. A Study in the Syntactic Use of the H- locale in Classical Hebrew* (1981):31, n.83 (on this important work see n. 32 below). H. takes אַרְצָה in the locative-terminal sense because to his mind, this word always has a locative-terminal function, cf. op. cit., p. 144. I would in this connection draw attention to אַרְצָה (accusative as locative, without the article) and הַשָּׁמַיְמָה (ה locale, locative-terminative, with the article) in Gen 28:12, etymologically and functionally different from each other ('set *on the ground* .... reaching *to the sky*' , E. A. Speiser, *Genesis* [The Anchor Bible, 1964]:217). To the above examples might be added נֹפֵל אַרְצָה 'lying on the ground' (Jud 3:25) and הַקִּים בְּבֵלָה (Jer 25:19). I prefer taking these forms as accusatives, partly because of the lack of movement and direction, and partly because of the wide-spread use of the accusative case as a locative in both East and West Semitic. Cf. also וַיִּכְרְעוּ אַפַּיִם אַרְצָה עַל־הָרִצְפָה (2 Chron 7:3) where אַרְצָה is best taken as an accusative (locative) as part of the circumstantial phrase אַפַּיִם אַרְצָה elaborated in the prepositional (stationary) phrase עַל־הָרִצְפָה. We have here (to use Hoftijzer's terminology in the book referred to above) an endocentric constituent consisting of two paratactic (pleonastic) elements which both have a *locative* function. There are a few instances in biblical Hebrew where אַרְצָה does not mean 'to the ground', but 'on the ground', or just 'the ground', 'the land', 'the earth' (accusative), *pace* Hoftijzer, op. cit., pp. 41, 42.

neither Ugaritic nor Hebrew, incidentally, is the suffix ever attached to living creatures of any kind. The reason for this may be that the semantic component of local fixedness[11] common to words for 'house', 'tent', 'altar' etc. is absent from words for animate objects. The accusative was more versatile and its function was not subject to such restrictions and could be used with persons in the local sense, certainly after verbs of motion (cf. e.g. the -אֶת construction in 2 Kgs 11:19). The local function of the demonstrative suffix proved too specific to become a structural feature of the language as a whole.

As has been said above, the Ugaritic suffix was probably the demonstrative suffix /ha/, attached to its noun by means of a binding vowel which is likely to have been /a/, if not actually the accusative ending, then at least identical with it.[12] The Ugaritic word for 'to the ground', therefore, may reasonably be reconstructed as *ʾárṣaha which in Hebrew was shortened to *ʾárṣa.[13] Hebrew, like Ugaritic, originally (i.e. during the pre-biblical period) possessed the two distinct suffixes -- the kinetic, enclitic particle /ha/ and the accusa-tive case ending /a/; the directional function of the proto-Semitic demonstrative particle /ha/ appears to have been peculiar to some NW Semitic dialects and Ethiopic.[14] The use of the simple accusative as a locative, on the other hand, is amply attested in the Semitic langauges, and it was for that reason that the older generation of philologists equated the ה locale (whose originally consonantal character they could know nothing about) with the accusative ending. In view of the Ugaritic evidence we need to address the question whether, in biblical Hebrew, the old accusative ending is preserved, both where the ending /a/ is used

---

11. The phraseology used here is J. Hoftijzer's. Cf. e.g. op. cit. p. 35.

12. For a discussion about the etymology of the connecting vowel, see J. Barth, in *American Journal of Semitic Languages*, 17 (1901):193ff. and A. Ungnad, in *Zeitschrift für Assyriologie* 17 (1903):333ff. and 18 (1904):1ff.

13. Cf. R. Meyer, *Hebräische Grammatik* (1969), para. 45, 3 (c); K. Aartun, *Die Partikeln des Ugaritischen* (1974), I, p.41. Both these philologists regard the /a/ before the demonstrative particle as the accusative ending, cf. also C. Gordon, op. cit., p. 112, who speaks of an 'accusative of goal', as distinct from the suffix /h/. J. Hoftijzer avoids speaking of the accusative and regards the local terminative function to be lodged in the enclitic particle, and not in any form of the noun to which the suffix is attached, in other words: to him the /a/ is nothing more than a connecting vowel, cf. his remarks in *Ugarit-Forschungen* 12 (1980):456. Cf. n. 6 above.

14. Cf. Dillmann, op. cit., p. 320, as regards the position in Ethiopic.

locatively and directionally (especially after verbs of motion),[15] and where it appears to be used with some syntactical function, either as a genuine feature of the spoken language, or as a late literary device used by authors long after the disappearance of the case endings.[16]

As has been said above, the loss of the enclitic /h/ construction in Hebrew probably occurred early, i.e. before the case endings had disappeared and before the accentual shift had occurred whereby the tone fell on the binding vowel and not on the root of the noun;[17] and the retention of the final, unstressed vowel functioning as a kinetic and directional indicator after the loss of the full, consonantal morpheme was possible because the vocalic suffix, formally identical with the accusative ending, which remained after the loss of the consonantal morpheme, was in itself sufficient to indicate not only location, but also, in some collocations, movement and direction. As may be seen in variations in MT[18] and in Qere-Kethib,[19] and in MT as compared

---

15. S. Moscati (ed.), op. cit., para 12.67, allows for this possibility; cf. also H. S. Nyberg, *Hebreisk Grammatik* (1952), para 56k, in accordance with the view of older grammarians.

16. Cf. n. 17 below.

17. For an early relative dating of these linguistic developments, see Z. S. Harris, *Development of the Canaanite Dialects* (1939): 42, 50. On the other hand, the Hebrew directional suffix is normally attached to the fully developed noun, not to the ground form (cf. n.2 above), a fact that can be observed most clearly in the segholates (עָרְיָה, בָּאֵרָה, קָדְמָה etc.). No linguistic feature of biblical Hebrew can be shown to have appeared or disappeared at a certain moment in time (Z. S. Harris). This would also apply to the accusative case ending. It would be strange if the Hebrew Bible, our main source of information about the structure of the NW Semitic languages, although largely reflecting a situation in which the case endings were lost, did not contain some evidence of survival of the accusative, either as genuine remains in ancient poetry, *or* in fixed phrases in later literary material (prose or poetry), or as deliberate archaisms introduced into poetry by poets who posessed knowledge of the earlier stage of the language when accusative forms were in common use, and made use of such forms in accordance with the syntactical rules of the language, with which they appear to have been familiar.

18. See e.g. 1 Sam 15:7, 27:8 [ה]שׁוּרָ בּוֹאֲךָ; 1 Sam 24:9, 1 Kgs 1:31 אֲפַיִם אַרְצָ[ה], N. B.: the shorter formula in Isa 49:23 is confirmed in 1QIsa[a]); 1 Kgs 8:22, 2 Chron 6:13 [ה]וַיִּפְרֹשׂ כַּפָּיו הַשָּׁמַיְמָ; Gen 46:3, Jos 24:4 יָרַד followed by מִצְרָיְמָ[ה]; 2 Kgs 25:3 הַמַּצָּפָה, Jer 40:6 הַמִּצְפָּתָה after בֹּא. נָפַל is followed by אֶרֶץ (Amos 9:9) and אַרְצָ[ה] (1 Sam 17:49), etc. etc. In Exod 8:20 we find the phrase בֵּיתָה

with Sam.[20] or with DSS material, notably of course the Great Isaiah scroll,[21] a noun indicating location or movement or direction towards a location may occur with or without the vocalic suffix, apparently with no difference in meaning.[22] This suggests that the original, consonantal suffix, if and when used in early Hebrew, was a variant of the noun in the accusative without the suffix, and that the speakers of Hebrew retained memory of the locative, kinetic, and directional functions of a word denoting some aspect of their (fixed) physical environment, even after the loss of the case ending.[23] Otherwise it would be difficult to account for the number of phrases where

---

פַּרְעֹה וּבֵית עֲבָדָיו after בּוֹא. Cf. n. 39 below.
  19. E.g. 1 Sam 9:26, where the suffixed form is preserved in the Qere (הַגָּגָה).
  20. As e.g. in Num 35:5 where MT reads קֵדְמָה...נֶגֶב...יָם...צָפוֹן, and Sam. קדמה...נגבה...ימה...צפונה.
  21. See E. Y. Kutscher, *The Language and Linguistic Background of the Isaiah Scroll* (1974):413f. In Isaiah 28:6 MT reads שַׁעְרָה and 1QIsaᵃ: שער.
  22. There may well have been instances in the spoken idiom of early Hebrew where the use or non-use of the directional suffix constituted a significant functional nuance, and it is not impossible that a thorough analysis of the verbs of motion e.g. from this point of view might yield some interesting results although there is enough evidence to suggest that, by and large, the use or non-use of the suffix made no difference in meaning. It is interesting to note that, although e.g. ירד as a verb of motion is frequently construed with a noun with the directional suffix attached, the specific idiom for 'those sailing on the high seas' is always יוֹרְדֵי הַיָּם, perhaps because the (unattested) יוֹרְדֵי הַיָּמָּה would, or could, mean 'those who sink into the sea'; we cannot be completely certain about this as the choice of e.g. שְׁאוֹלָה/שְׁאוֹל with ירד occurs with no difference in meaning, although it should be pointed out that the latter phrase always refers to '*descending to* S.', and never functions in a way strictly comparable to the idiomatic יוֹרְדֵי הַיָּם. In Obad 1:3 הוֹרִיד אֶרֶץ may well have a meaning substantially different from the one conveyed by הוֹרִיד אַרְצָה ('bring down to the land of...'); cf. n. 44 below. The lack of consistency in the scant evidence makes it difficult to reach firm conclusions. The attested constructions with אָסַף show an apparent lack of consistency: ה locale constructions are found *qal* and *piʿel*, but only once in *niphʿal* (Judg 20:14) where the normal construction is the (unmarked) accusative functioning as a locative. The reason for this difference in usage may be that in *niphʿal* the locative function was felt to be predominant.
  23. The אֶת־ phrases with local function in Hebrew prose texts would, I think, confirm some such view. Cf. n. 27 below.

the suffix /a/ might have been used, but was not in fact used.[24] It would, by the way be too simplistic to suggest that prepositions took the place of the accusative case as indicating location and movement towards a terminal. The proclitic prepositions /b/, /l/, (and also /ᶜd/) appear already in Ugaritic as alternatives to the enclitic /h/ and the accusative constructions,[25] and the three constructions are likely to have co-occurred in Hebrew also, already at the pre-biblical stage of the language,[26] in the same way as e.g. the accusative case ending /a/ and the accusative marker אֶת־ with the local function probably co-occurred in early Hebrew.[27]

---

24. For a list of such cases, see J. Hoftijzer, op. cit., p. 51f., n.154. Hoftijzer is well aware, of course, of the incompleteness not only of his list, but also of the literary remains on which his compilation is based. There are words which lack what H. calls 'a semantic component of local fixedness' (cf. n. 11 above) - words like שְׂמֹאל, יָמִין and סָבִיב. These words express fixedness only 'in relation to another object' and are therefore never construed with the directional suffix (op. cit., p. 53f., n. 160).

25. Without going into details, I would refer the interested reader to the following passages (in Gibson's edition, see n. 8 above): 14:63-63, 74, 108, 116-7, 123, 135; 23:10, 30, 37 where examples of the directional suffix /h/, the accusative and the prepositions /b/, /l/ and /ᶜd/ occur. To express 'place where' Ugaritic normally uses the accusative, or a preposition; to express 'place whereto' the directional suffix /h/, the accusative, or a preposition is used.

26. H. Ewald, *Syntax of the Hebrew Language of the Old Testament* (1881):43-71, in his fine chapter on 'the verb with the accusative and with prepositions', wisely desists from speculating on the relative chronology of these constructions; in some cases, they can be seen to be more than mere variations, however: in prepositional expressions there is sometimes a degree of precision and nuance which may be absent from a loosely applied accusative form, while in other cases the attested constructions may be synonymous, as e.g. in the case of פָּנֶה with דֶּרֶךְ, אֶל־דֶּרֶךְ or לְדֶרֶךְ with little or no difference in meaning.

27. There are not many cases of אֶת־ with a local function, most of them after verbs of motion; for a list see Hoftijzer, op. cit., p. 88, n. 275. A striking case occurs in 2 Kgs 11:19 וַיּוֹרִידוּ אֶת־הַמֶּלֶךְ 'and they brought down *to* the king'. The accusative with אֶת־ in the locative (stationary) sense is striking in 1 Sam 7:16 (אֶת כָּל הַמְּקוֹמוֹת הָאֵלֶּה '*in* all these places': the phrase cannot be taken as an object construction; and the reason for את here appears to be the memory of the accusative functioning as a locative, as in Ethiopic, Akkadian, Arabic, and Ugaritic.

The assumption of an early disappearance in Hebrew of the enclitic /h/ construction would account for the restricted and highly selective use of the final, unstressed /a/ of direction,[28] and the small number of instances in the Ras Shamra texts, coupled with its absence from the Phoenician inscriptions, suggests that the suffix in its directional function was a relatively insignificant and passing feature whose role in the linguistic history of Hebrew was to help preserve the old accusative ending which by itself was capable of functioning directionally and kinetically especially, of course, after verbs of motion, but also otherwise. The longer variant proved unnecessary and eventually fell out of use; and in biblical Hebrew there is no evidence of it -- only of the vocalic suffix which the older grammarians, as has been said above, regarded as the accusative ending.[29] So, the spelling in MT is conventional, and the ה is a *mater lectionis* which should not itself be taken as pointing to an original enclitic /h/; and through a combination of syllable reduction and conventional scribal practice the Hebrew directional, kinetic particle appears in our texts as identical with and indistinguishable from the accusative case ending which had a variety of syntactical and adverbial functions, in addition to the locative and local-terminative functions which it shared with the enclitic, consonantal particle. This linguistic development, resulting from the merger of an original, specifically spatial and kinetic particle with the less specific and more versatile case ending, is an indication of extreme linguistic economy, compared with e.g. Finnish which posesses nine 'local' cases, of which three, apart from spatial and kinetic functions, posess

---

28. For a discussion of these matters, see Hoftijzer, op. cit., pp. 238ff., 243ff.

29. However the memory of the specifically directional function of the demonstrative suffix survived in some types of ancient Hebrew prose writings. In poetry the situation is different; in Hoftijzer's words: 'not only is the noun with the /a/ suffix used .... [in poetry] where it would not have been used in prose, it is never used in poetic material in those instances where it could or would have been used in prose' op. cit., p. 163). The ending /a/ appears in poetry without any trace of a locative or directional function (for a list, see Hoftijzer, op. cit., p. 162), and all such instances are excluded from Hoftijzer's monograph on the ה locale for that reason. It would not, in my view, be unreasonable to suppose that some evidence of the accusative ending may be found in such instances (see already F. Böttcher, op. cit., para. 615d, n. 3); and I would allow for the possibility of deliberate introduction of ancient grammatical features (such as e.g. the accusative) even into late texts (cf. n. 17 above). In some instances the ending can be seen to have a grammatical function; it was more than just 'some kind of literary device' (against Hoftijzer, op. cit., pp. 215, 247).

syntactical and adverbial functions as well.[30] In Hebrew, however, the specifically 'local' case, or the memory of it, survived in some types of ancient prose writings, attached to a few proper names and common nouns which all have a common semantic content. In both East and West Semitic spatial and kinetic function could be expressed either by the accusative case, or by an enclitic particle(/ha/ in Ugaritic and Hebrew and /iš/ in East Semitic), or by a preposition; in Hebrew these three alternatives were reduced to two through the elimination of the original morphological difference between the local case and the accusative. The accusative /a/ thus proved the stronger of the two originally different speech elements, and it is not unreasonable to suppose that some evidence of it, with syntactical and adverbial functions, may be found in MT. There is, in my opinion, more evidence in biblical Hebrew of the accusative ending than of, say, the enclitic *mem*. Of the latter there may perhaps be half a dozen or so convincing instances, but of the accusative there are considerably more although recent grammars are virtually silent on the subject.[31]

---

30. Cf. M. Branch, in *The World's Major Languages* (ed. B. Comrie, cf. n. 2 above), pp. 609ff.

31. That applies e.g. to R. Meyer's Grammar (cf. n. 13 above) which does not contain a single example of the accusative case ending occurring with a grammatical function in sentences, although there are instances of this, as recognized in the older grammars, see e.g. *G.K.* para. 90f and n. 7 above. E. A. Speiser also in his interesting article (referred to in n. 3 above) has nothing to say about the accusative, but that is because the purpose of his article is to trace the etymology, not of the accusative, but of the local suffix. The old accusative ending has been detected by M. Dahood in a number of instances in Hebrew poetry, especially the Psalms, see his *Psalms III* (1970):381 for some examples. Dahood's pupils have, with varying degrees of success, claimed to have discovered other examples. One of the persuasive instances occurs in Nahum 2:14, see K. J. Cathcart, *Nahum in the Light of Northwest Semitic* (Biblia et Orientalia 26, 1973):109. That isolated words like לַיְלָה (cf. n. 4 above), עַתָּה etc. are etymologically accusative forms has been recognized for a long time and needs no particular documentation; and נַחְלָה as used in Ps 124:4, was correctly described as an adverbial accusative by Böttcher, op. cit., p. 629, cf. also M. Dahood (presumably independently), op. cit., p. 212, who points to the accusative forms occurring particularly in the Psalms of Ascent. A very interesting case on the adverbial accusative has turned up in the D.S.S. where the form מָאדָה occurs with great frequency, to the virtual exclusion of מְאֹד in biblical Hebrew. (For details I must refer you to my forthcoming article in the *Vermès Festschrift* to be published later this year). J. Hoftijzer, op. cit., p. 165 has made the ingenious suggestion that the difficult פְּנִימָה in Ps 45:14 (which H. reads as *pānī́mā*) be taken to mean 'as to countenance/ap-

There are some interesting cases of the accusative case functioning syntactically in sentences which deserve a place in historical grammars of the Hebrew language. In what follows I shall not deal with those many ambivalent cases in which the directional /a/ cannot be distinguished with certainty from the accusative, especially after verbs of motion, although much could be said on this topic; I am convinced that many of the constructions after verbs of motion will, by careful study, turn out to be case constructions, rather than local-terminative /a/ constructions. However this may be, in the present context I am more concerned with a few unusual features in MT which can be explained as syntactical structures in which a word appears in the accusative, with the case ending, either as the subject, predicate, or the object of a sentence. My examples are gleaned from poetry and prose, and are not confined to words like מַרְתָה, יְשׁוּעָתָה, אֵימָתָה, צָרָתָה, עֶזְרָתָה, עוֹלָתָה etc. where the unstressed final /a/ is commonly held to be identical with ה locale, but without meaning. However, as it is clear that the above and similar words are semantically quite different from the words in the prose texts to which the directional /a/ is attached, it would be advisable to distinguish between the two endings and to explain the suffix, where appropriate, as the accusative ending, and to seek a syntactic explanation for its occurrence, either as a surviving feature of the language, or as a literary device employed by the biblical writers.[32]

---

pearance', a sense that can only be arrived at if the word is described as an (adverbial) accusative, although H. does not use the term.

32. J. Hoftijzer, in his monograph (cf. n. 10 above) presents a formal, synchronic constituent analysis of the ה locale in different types of Hebrew sentence structures; and by disregarding the philological evidence, which suggests a number of different origins for the final, unstressed /a/, and concentrating on formal, syntactic structures to the exclusion of a paradigmatic study of word variation, he eliminates the confusion to be seen in some of our dictionaries (such as B.D.B. and K.B.). H. equates the endings of אַרְצָה and אֲקוּמָה (op. cit., p. 6) but excludes the verbal ending from the enquiry. In actual fact, he does not apply the formal, analytical principle in its purity, as he often appeals to meaning and frequently discusses exegetical matters to define the precise function of the ending in the context of a sentence as a whole. H. is, of course, not unaware of the varied background of the local suffix; he was even planning to write an article about the /h/ morpheme and the accusative case (op. cit., p. 220 n. 654), a project later abandoned (communication by letter to the present writer). Although H. is thus aware of the possibility that there are instances of the accusative, he makes no attempt in his book to distinguish between the directional suffix and the case ending, and by excluding all cases where the ending does not function directionally or

Already B. Stade spoke of 'ziemlich umfangreiche Trümmer eines Accusatives auf â', and referred to the survival of the case ending in the construct state of some nouns, as e.g. in בֵּיתָה־יּוֹסֵף, בָּאֲרָה שֶׁבַע, מִדְבָּרָה הַמֶּשֶׁק.[33] If one accepts the originally longer, consonantal structure of the directional morpheme one might well doubt whether that suffix was ever attached to Hebrew nouns in the construct state, and whether phrases like the above (occurring after verbs of motion) should not rather be described as accusative constructions.[34] The same would apply to e.g. וַיִּתְקָעֵהוּ יָמָּה סּוּף (Exod 10:19) 'and drove them (i.e. the locusts) into the Red Sea'.[35] It is important to note that in Ugaritic the directional suffix is never attached

---

locatively, *de facto* disregards the possibility of the ending functioning syntactically as a case marker; and he avoids the term 'accusative' altogether: such a term would suggest a syntactic relationship at clause level which is outside H.s concern. His monograph combines modern linguistics (formal, synchronic approach) and biblical scholarship (source-analysis, exegesis). H. recognizes, of course, that the biblical texts are not all from the same period.

33. Op. cit., paras. 342 a.d. For the use of accusative after verbs of motion in Arabic, see H. Reckendorf, *Die syntaktischen Verhältnisse des Arabischen* (1898):96, and his *Arabische Syntax* (1921):75. -- פַּדֶּנָה אֲרָם (Gen 28:2), after a verb of motion (הָלַךְ) should be added to Stade's list as פַּדָּן was not originally a proper name but an appellative, and the construction is similar to בָּאֲרָה שֶׁבַע. In 2 Sam 24:6 (דָּנָה יַעַן), also after a verb of motion (בּוֹא), the assumption of a ה locale is difficult; the text is usually corrected (cf. B.D.B., p.193). Given the clear evidence in Ugaritic texts of case endings attached to nouns in the construct state, the observations made in H. Bauer/P. Leander, *Historische Grammatik der hebräischen Sprache des Alten Testaments* (1922), para. 65d are no longer valid. Hoftijzer. op. cit., p. 48, n. 142, describes, in my view incorrectly, the phrase מִדְבָּרָה בֵּית אָוֶן (Josh 18:12) as 'an endocentric constituent consisting of two paratactic elements' (towards the desert, to B.-A.). H. is well aware, of course, that the usual taking of מִדְבָּרָה as *nomen regens* is indicated by the accents used here. H. deals with מִדְבָּרָה הַמֶּשֶׁק (op. cit., p. 48, n. 143) in a similar fashion.

34. Cf. also אַרְצָה כְּנַעַן (Gen 12:5, 31:18), אַרְצָה בְנֵי־קֶדֶם (Gen 29:1) after verbs of motion.

35. Apart from being, in the above cases, attached to a *nomen regens*, the ending /a/ can be attached to the *nomen rectum* of a construct connection, cf. e.g. עַל דֶּרֶךְ תִּמְנָתָה. This longer form of תִּמְנָה occurs also after the preposition בּ (Judg 14:1) and is perhaps to be explained as the accusative form which lost its original function and became an alternative form of תִּמְנָה, in the same way as e.g. יַהְצָה appears to have become an alternative form of יַהַץ, cf. בְּיַהְצָה (Judg 11:20), and probably also בְּבָלָה,

to a word in the construct state.

There are, as has already been mentioned, cases in which an accusative form with the case ending preserved can be seen to fulfil a syntactical function.[36] In this connection one thinks immediately, of course, of simple object constructions. The material is not large, but nevertheless significant enough to be included in a historical treatment of biblical Hebrew. In a few cases final /a/ does indeed appear to occur as an object indicator in a sentence. Thus in Gen 27:3 וְצוּדָה לִּי צֵידָה 'hunt some venison for me' (Speiser), the full cognate accusative is preserved in the Kethib (צידה), cf. v.33 and Gen 25:28.[37] Another very interesting case occurs in Gen 49:15: וַיַּרְא מְנֻחָה כִּי טוֹב וְאֶת הָאָרֶץ כִּי נָעֵמָה. In this line the masc. form טוֹב does not agree with the fem. form of מְנֻחָה, but this difficulty is resolved by reading the accusative form of מָנוֹחַ (i.e. manṓḫa or manū́ḫa), with no difference in meaning and in perfect parallelism with verse 15b. We have here an early case of the poet making use of both accusative constructions in parallel structures.[38] In Jer 48:19 נָס שַׁאֲלִי וְנִמְלָטָה rhymes with the following אִמְרִי מַה נִּהְיָתָה, the form נִמְלָטָה being the

---

as in מְבָבֶלָה (Jer 27:16). Cf. n.1 above.

36. For some examples, see *Journal of Semitic Studies*, 33 (1988):161. Most of the material presented there is not a result of my own original research, but is referred to simply for the purpose of giving some indication of the work done by scholars in this area. Cf. also J. Hoftijzer, op. cit., p. 156ff., where an analysis of the (poetic and non-narrative prophetic) relevant material may be found.

37. See n. 38 below.

38. It is very interesting to see אֶת־ used here (in an ancient line of poetry), in its original capacity of an emphatic particle, for the purpose of climax in the second half of the line. I would suggest that spoken Hebrew at the time this line was composed posessed both the accusative ending and the particle אֶת־, the latter being used for emphasis and rhetorical and stylistic effect. The simple accusative ending could be employed for a similar purpose (cf. Gen 27:3 mentioned above, where the fuller form ṣayĕdā is rhetorically far more effective that the simple צֵיד ; and yet the Kethib is uniformly rejected by all modern scholars, except M. Dahood, who was well aware of the case ending /a/ in biblical Hebrew, and identified צֵידָה, מְנֻחָה (Gen 49:15) and other words in the Bible as object accusatives, see *Biblica* 48(i), [1967]:427f., and 58 [1977]:423). In Jer 48:19 mentioned below, we have another very fine case of an accusative form being employed for the sake of rhetorical effect (and rhyme).

accusative of the masc. נִמְלָט.[39] Other straight object accusatives occur in Jer 11:15 (הַמְזִמָּתָה); Hos 8:7 (סוּפָתָה, cf. G.K. para. 90f); 10:13 (עָרְלָתָה); cf. Ps 8:8 (צֹנֶה)[40] and Ps 68:7 (בִּיחוֹתָה).[41] In Nah 1:8 (כָלָה יַעֲשֶׂה מְקוֹמָהּ) máqōma (accus. of מָקוֹם) should be read, the fem. suffix being without reference, and מָקוֹם (here probably functioning as a collective noun 'enemies', parallel with the following (וְאֹיְבָיו) being the object of the compound verb כָּלָה עָשָׂה 'destroy'.[42] Sometimes an interesting

---

39. All the ancient versions translate נִמְלָטָה by masculine, parallel with נָס. R.S.V. reflects the putative feminine form 'ask him who flees and her who escapes'. B.D.B. makes the startling suggestion that וְנִמְלָטָה is the 3rd fem. consecutive perfect. There is, incidentally, nothing remarkable in the suffix /a/ being used in one, and not in both, of two words occurring together, with the same syntactical function: for variations of this kind in the same verse, see e.g. שְׁכֶמָה and שְׁכֶם in 2 Chron 10:1, after הָלַךְ and בּוֹא; (in 1 Kgs 12:1 שְׁכֶם is used twice);cf. also תַּרְשִׁישָׁה and תַּרְשִׁישׁ in Jer 40:12 and Jon 1:3; after בּוֹא the phrase בִּיתָה פַּרְעֹה is combined in parallelism with וּבֵית עֲבָדָיו in Exod 8:20. In Hab 1:16 בְּרִיאָה of MT (1QpHab: ברי) is not a feminine form (against A. Sperber, The Premasoretic Bible. A Grammar of Masoretic Hebrew [1959]:145): after שָׁמֵן and as the predicate of מַאֲכָלוֹ, בריאה should be read as bārī'āh, accusative of ברי.

40. Cf. Dahood, Psalms I (1965):51, after D. N. Freedman). The correction of צֹנֶה to צֹאנָה (Dahood) is not necessary as final /a/ can undergo a change in the direction of Seghol, after certain 'soft' consonants, /n/ being one of them, see already Böttcher, op. cit., p. 404, where reference is made to forms like אָנָה and יָרְשֶׁנָה. To Böttcher's list one could add נָבֶה (1 Sam 21:2) equivalent to נָבָה (see G.K. 90i; E. Dhorme, Les livres de Samuel [1910]:193, correctly describes the form as a locative [after בּוֹא]). B.L., p. 456 wrongly takes צֹנָה as a feminine form. For other cases of an original accusative form mistakenly being taken as a feminine form, see notes 1 and 39 above. The D.S.S. form מאו(ר)דה in MT, see n. 31 above) was also commonly regarded as a feminine form in the 1950's and 1960's.

41. On this passage see J.S.S. 33 (1988):161 and the references to literature quoted there. The phrase לְהוֹרֹת לְפָנָיו גֹּשְׁנָה (Gen 46:28) is perhaps a little awkward 'to show before him' G. (or the way to G.). On the face of it we seem to have the directional suffix in גֹּשְׁנָה, but not necessarily: after לְהוֹרֹת (Sam. להוראות) it could be the accusative form of גֹּשֶׁן; the following אַרְצָה גֹּשֶׁן is certainly accusative (cf n. 33 above) and גֹּשְׁנָה in v.32 is non-directional and probably accusative.

42. For compound verbs of this kind, capable of taking a (second) direct object, see A. B. Davidson, Hebrew Syntax (1901):111, Rem. 7. With עָשָׂה כָּלָה this type of construction is clearly seen in Jer 30:11, 46:28; Ezek 11:13, 20:17; Zeph 1:18, Neh 9:31, and probably also in Jer 5:18 where, according to MT, the preposition אֵת־ 'with' is used;

ambiguity can arise. In 2 Kgs 13:18 e.g. אַרְצָה functions as the object of הַךְ ('strike the ground') and is clearly the accusative of אֶרֶץ (the phrase is the equivalent of אֶת הַךְ וְ עֲפַר הָאָרֶץ in Exod 8:12); but in 2 Sam 2:22 the same phrase means 'strike *to* the ground' (='kill'), the verbal form being construed with a pronominal suffix followed by אֶרֶץ with the directional suffix;[43] in Isaiah 11:4 the same phrase, *without* the directional suffix (וְהִכָּה אֶרֶץ) functions as a compound verb parallel with the following יָמִית and capable of taking a direct object, viz. רָשָׁע at the end of the line;[44] the use of the *maqqef* suggests that the punctuators realized the compound nature of this verb which, like similar compound verbs (cf. n. 42 above) can be construed with a direct object.

The directional /a/ and the accusative ending are both found in the early biblical prose texts, whereas the directional /a/ is absent from biblical poetry.[45] However, the latter contains evidence of the accusative ending, both in object constructions, and in other syntactical structures. Let me mention two areas in particular, with a few illustrative examples taken from prose and poetry.

The first concerns the predicate in verbal sentences with הָיָה 'to be', and in nominal sentences without הָיָה. In Jos 17:9 (הַיָּמָּה תֹּצְאוֹתָיו וַיְהִי) and Jos 18:12 (אָרֶן בֵּית מִדְבָּרָה תֹּצְאוֹתָיו וְהָיָה) the suffix in הַיָּמָּה and מִדְבָּרָה respectively is the accusative case ending marking the predicate after הָיָה; cf. Ps 63:8 כִּי־הָיִיתָה לִּי עֶזְרָתָה. Without the finite verb, in a nominal sentence, we find הַיָּמָּה similarly used in Jos 15:12, and עֶזְרָתָה in Ps 94:17. Comparable structures are found in classical Arabic.[46]

The second function in which the accusative case construction can be seen to occur with syntactical function concerns a feature of Hebrew sentence structure which

---

for a discussion about מְקוֹמָהּ in Nah 1:8, see K. J. Cathcart, op. cit., p. 57f.

43. In the spoken language the two phrases were probably originally distinguished by using ᵓárṣa and ᵓárṣaʰ respectively, cf. the remarks in n. 22 above.

44. The true parallelism in this beautifully structured verse is blurred if וְהִכָּה אֶרֶץ is taken to mean 'and he shall smite the earth' (R.S.V.).

45. הַמָּוְתָה in Ps 116:15 was mistakenly taken by E. König and others in the sense 'die Preisgabe in den Tod'; for a detailed examination of the syntactical structure of that passage, cf. *J.S.S.* 33 (1988):155ff.

46. Cf. H. Reckendorf *Die Syntaktischen Verhältnisse*, p. 104ff.; and his *Syntax*, pp.100ff.

has been largely neglected by grammarians. I am referrring to the use of the accusative as a marker of the semantic impersonal subject in verbal or nominal sentences. It appears that, in such cases, the subject is formally an attribute, specifying the implied subject of the verb, or a qualifying noun and therefore marked as an accusative of specification.[47] If there is a finite verb it may be in the simplest form (3rd m.s.), or it may agree in gender and number with the semantic subject. In Ezek 28:15: (עַד־נִמְצָא עַוְלָתָה בָּךְ) עַוְלָתָה (accusative of עַוְלָה [fem.]) is the subject of נִמְצָא (masc.); the same phrase occurs in Mal 2:6 without the accusative marker, and with the feminine subject *preceding* the masculine verb. The tendency to eliminate apparent incongruence of this kind may be seen e.g. in אֵימָתָה .... תִּפֹּל (Exod 15:16).[48]

The form קָוֵה (for קָו 'measuring line') occurs three times in the Kethib of MT (1 Kgs 7:23, Jer 31:39, Zech 1:16). The word is given a separate entry in the dictionaries although in all three passages it can be taken as the accusative of קָו, twice in the construct (1 Kgs 7:23, Jer 31:39) and once in the absolute state (Zech 1:16); in all three passages the word is construed with a 3rd m.s. verb, either preceding or following the semantic subject. The word קָו is presumably masculine, although we cannot deduce this from these three passages, as the word functions as the impersonal, semantic subject in the accusative of verbs in 3rd m.s. (The vocalization of the Kethib as קָוֶה or קָוֵה, constr. קְוֵה can probably be dispensed with, and the word should perhaps not be given a separate entry in the dictionaries).

In the above observations I have confined myself to giving a brief survey and dicussion of what is, in fact, a very complex problem in Hebrew Grammar. Although,

---

47. Cf. my remarks, art. cit. (see n. 45 above), p. 163. S. de Sacy, *Grammaire Arabe II* (1905):59, although quoting some examples of this usage from the Qur'an and elsewhere, queries the correctness of this construction and reads the nominative in all cases.

48. Sam., by reading אֵימָה, has completed the process of simplification by eliminating the accusative form of the semantic subject. A similar tendency to eliminate constructions of this kind can be observed elsewhere in MT, see *J.S.S.*, art. cit., (cf, n. 45 above) p. 163f. In nominal sentences with אַיִן and לֹא the semantic subject is in the accusative in e.g. Ps 3:3 (אֵין יְשׁוּעָתָה), Ps 92:16 (Qere וְלֹא עַוְלָתָה), Ps 94:17 (לוּלֵי יהוה עֶזְרָתָה לִּי). There are close parallels in classical Arabic to these constructions which are akin to the verbal and nominal sentences (with and without היה) mentioned above.

admittedly, there are not many instances of preservation of the old accusative ending, there is enough evidence in MT to warrant the reinstatement of this linguistic feature in treatments of historical Hebrew syntax, whether prose or poetry. Philologists are becoming increasingly aware of the need for separate treatments of Hebrew syntax in prose and poetry; in the former the accusative is sporadically preserved, possibly as remains of the spoken language; in the latter it is often more correctly described as a late, artificial feature, a literary device deliberately introduced into compositions (in accordance with the rules of grammar with which the biblical poets were familiar), for euphonic or rhetorical effect, or for reasons of metre or rhyme, or both. In prose the problem is largely to determine the true nature of the /a/ ending -- whether it is the ה locale proper (in the directional sense), or the accusative ending indicating the 'place where' or, after verbs of motion (as the direct object of such verbs) the 'place whither'. *That* problem at least does not apply in poetry; there the ending, although identical in form with the directional ending, should in all cases be explained differently, viz. as a case ending which in a number of instances, though not in all, can be seen to fulfill a syntactical function. Where that does not appear to be the case, it is necessary to suppose that the accusative ending (like the ה locale) eventually lost its functional character, as was pointed out in the beginning of this article.

www.ingramcontent.com/pod-product-compliance
Lightning Source LLC
Chambersburg PA
CBHW032300150426
43195CB00008BA/518